Evolving To Be Me

Kissing Death and Trusting Myself

Debra Rachar

Evolving To Be Me

Kissing Death and Trusting Myself

Debra Rachar
Author | Positive Energy Generator | Survivor

*Thank you lucky Scaro!
Many Blessings
With Love
Debra Rachar*

Published by EmptyPens Publishing
May 2022 ISBN: 9781778185007

Copyright © 2022 by Debra Rachar
All rights reserved. No part of this publication may be reproduced, stored in, or introduced into a retrieval system, or transmitted, in any form, or by any means (electronic, mechanical, photocopying, recording or otherwise) without the prior written permission of the publisher. This book is sold subject to the condition that it shall not, by way of trade or otherwise, be lent, resold, hired out, or otherwise circulated without the publisher's prior consent in any form of binding or cover other than that in which it is published and without a similar condition including this condition being imposed on the subsequent purchaser.

Editor: Diana Reyers
Typeset: Greg Salisbury
Book Cover Design: Olli Vidal

DISCLAIMER: Readers of this publication agree that Debra Rachar will not be held responsible or liable for damages that may be alleged as resulting directly or indirectly from the use of this publication. The publisher/author cannot be held accountable for the information provided by, or actions, resulting from, accessing these resources.

Dedication

For all my family

*And for every person who has helped me
learn the lessons I needed to learn.*

*And for anyone who hasn't felt worthy
or enough and has lost their voice.*

*It is my hope that you find your recipe
to evolve and become your authentic self.*

A portion of the profits from the sale of this book will be
donated to The Happy Liver Society.

Testimonials

Debra writes in her personal version of *Four B's of What Makes a Person Feel Worthy*—I know I have a positive effect on those I interact with. I can attest to the truth in that statement. I know that I won the lottery when my brother married this beautiful woman.

Debra tells a compelling story of her life journey. The hard lessons of being a child of an addicted parent, the normal (and not so normal) challenges that come with being a wife and mother, and most certainly her health issues and not one - but two - liver transplants.

Debra frankly describes her feelings and her experiences, with no expectation of special treatment and never asking for our pity. She shows her commitment to finding her best life, taking us along for the ride—sharing generously the lessons she has learned, as well as a treasure trove of reading material, quotes and music titles so we can explore her resources for ourselves.

Debra gives us a useful primer for being present for your own life, paying attention, celebrating the wins and naming the losses. Thank you.

Pearl Rebecca Wittman
RN, B. *Adm*

Everyone has a story to tell; some are just more motivated to put it into print. Debra's passion to tell her story in a brutally honest, courageous way left me wondering why I did not truly know her and her journey through a troubled, at times, traumatized childhood, her marriage struggles, financial struggles, and the biggest physical struggle of her life.....

As I read through her manuscript, I identified with a lot of her childhood struggles. It was like I was seeing myself as a child all over again. Debra's quest for life and her hunger for self-improvement inspire me. She has overcome so much adversity and has accomplished many great feats over the past few decades. Her tenacious yet comforting spirit came to light as she penned her amazing journey called *Life*. I am truly honoured to have her as a sister-in-law, but more so, a friend! She is indeed my Warrior Princess

Linda Jackson Rachar
Retired Chiropractic Office Assistant

Having the privilege to contribute to the sharing of someone's story is a blessing I reap the rewards from every day. Part of my goal as an editor is to enhance the message the author strives to articulate within their memoir while maintaining their style. Each theme, common thread, and epiphanic reflection they mindfully incorporate must be highlighted in a way that heightens the awareness of the author's message.

Debra Rachar's *Evolving To Be Me: Kissing Death and Trusting Myself* is filled with such inspirational insights and lessons. This can only be done through brave storytelling—the kind that connects the reader to meaningful emotion and raw, vulnerable truths. How does one share what it was like as a daughter of an alcoholic parent while simultaneously including their unconditional love for them? How does one move through the trauma of a double liver transplant and hold their family together? How does one achieve a degree of vulnerability that only the very brave are willing to spill on the page and then confidently share with the world?

I believe Ms. Rachar clarified what integrity meant to her and used it as a powerful guide behind her cathartic writing process. She knew what she proudly wanted to share in order to support others and did it in a way that respected all the key players in her story. This is an account of unconditional love for self and others—the depth of love that only someone landing in the trenches of personal deceit can eventually achieve if they are willing to open their soul to the truth.

Diana Reyers, Author
Around the Table: Escaping the Cycle of Insanity
Founder, Daring to Share Global™

The authenticity and complete vulnerability that Debra courageously embraces throughout the anecdotal recounting of her life's journey is reflected in this eloquent memoir, evoking inspiration and providing a riveting read! Her telling is infused with heart and unabridged devotion to her truth.

The journey through her myriad of experiences—murky and lustrous, daunting and sanguine—is so clearly articulated and resonates deeply within my soul as I submerge. All the boxes checked: military upbringing, child of an alcoholic father, 12-step journey (ACOA), feelings of inadequacy, unworthiness and imposter syndrome, losing myself in a marriage, giving away my power…and the parallel continues.

Debra negotiates her personal trek through intense introspection and a fierce devotion to personal growth, seeking development toward her highest self. Her uplifting attitude and stellar drive forward, against all odds, is a testament to exemplar resilience! It is clear that her inner fire continues to blaze—with heartfelt generosity and dedication. Debra has skillfully crafted her memoir to maximize the positive impact upon her audience as her earnest intent to help others shines through.

An absolute must-read!

Brenda Scatterty
Financial Administrator,
University of Alberta,
Professional/Freelance Writer/Editor

With integrity, authenticity and compassion, Debra courageously explores her past, sensitively describes today, and is eternally grateful for a bright tomorrow.

In this moving memoir, she shares her memories, thoughts, and dreams with generosity and grace, finding lessons from life's teaching moments. She researches, shares recipes for reflection, pays attention to details and speaks her truth. She lets her light shine and has learned that she does not do the world any favours by playing small.

Debra, I see you from here, my friend. Take one more step.

Pamela MacDonald
Climbing Partner & Travel Coach

In this very unique and deeply personal memoir, Debra opens her heart and bares her soul to tell us of her growing up with an alcoholic father, coping with lifelong mental and physical illness, and cheating death. Her recipes for healing and forgiveness are a treasure, a gift indeed, a template for you! You will learn much from reading this courageous memoir. I felt true joy at Debra's success and incredible accomplishments.

Colleen Marshall
Wise Trusted Friend

How does a person overcome adversity in their life, manage to move through difficult circumstances without being crushed by them, take the enlightenment that was gleaned from surviving that challenge, and share that light with others? Deb Rachar courageously writes about her most difficult life stories. She brings the reader through the stories without traumatizing them, reflects on the lessons learned each time, and then shares the questions she asks herself in the aftermath. Her ability to reflect on her experiences and share her wisdom in her writing shows a tremendous generosity of spirit. This book illustrates how personal growth doesn't just change your own life; it changes the lives of those around you.

I found myself reading each chapter as though I was reading a fictional novel, eager to find out what happened next! Though I have known Deb for many years, even while she lived through many of the events she recounts here, I found so much insight into how she spins gold from barbed wire and how she has achieved her tremendous resilience.

Deb inspires us firstly by courageously sharing her life stories and secondly with her personal growth that she has diligently and persistently worked on throughout all of her life's obstacles.

Her story is about facing death and how she got there, about learning to live authentically and learning to trust herself. She shows the reader through her stories how to live with compassion and appreciation. And she doesn't just share her stories—she shines a light to show the reader how they too can create awareness, intention, and resilience in their own lives.

Anne Morris
Fellow Toastmaster and Supportive Friend

Gratitude

First and foremost, to my husband and soulmate, you have always believed in me and loved me just as I am. We have had our ups and downs and have weathered the storms together. We have learned to grow together and strengthen our love and commitment to each other with each changing year. Your love and support have allowed me to find my voice, learn lessons and grow physically, mentally, and spiritually. You have been my greatest teacher, and knowing that you always had my back has enabled me to change my beliefs, stories, and old patterns of thinking.

To my two grown children, thank you for always believing in and supporting me at every turn. We went through many changes together, many moves and many days of uncertainty. We became stronger and learned so much from each other and strengthened our relationship through listening, sharing and being honest with each other. You always knew if I had to line up all the little girls or boys and pick only one for my daughter or son, it would be you because you are very special to me. You both light up my life.

To all my family who always believed in me, supported me through thick and thin, and loved me just the way I was and am, thank you for being with me on this adventure through sickness and health and now having a deeper connection and being stronger emotionally together. I love each of you to the moon and back.

Thank you to the many friends who supported me in countless ways, at work, to explore travel, at toastmasters, to dream big and not play small, and who believed in me and inspired me to write this memoir. I appreciate all of you who supported me through my liver transplant journey and beyond with your love, time, cards, gifts, taking care of my dog, offering my family a place to stay, and always being there on the other end of the phone or computer. Each one of you has played a significant part in me becoming more authentic.

To all the staff at Vancouver General Hospital in the transplant ward, each of you cared for me and made my day, from the cleaning staff, porters, kitchen staff, laboratory technicians doing blood work at 6:00 a.m. to the nurses with the patience of a saint, the therapists, social workers, and physiotherapists. To the surgeons and doctors who saved my life by making difficult decisions and supporting me and my family through some very challenging medical situations.

To Karen Stacey, who founded the Happy Liver Foundation and opened Stacey House, you gave our family and friends a home away from home while staying in Vancouver during my liver transplant recovery. My family and I will be forever grateful for your kindness and support.

To Diana Reyers, thank you for your wisdom, patience, guidance, and dedication to your passion for helping others share their stories. I really appreciated you for editing my writing and story and for believing and helping me share my story with others. Thank you for trusting and inspiring me to be authentic within my desire to include quotes and recipes in a memoir. Thank you for co-writing Daring to Share Your Story as a guide to help me and others write their memoir. I am overjoyed to have met you.

To you, the reader, thank you for being interested in

reading my story and helping me spread the message that the past does not equal the future, and we can all evolve to become our authentic selves.

Foreword

I met Deb Rachar at a time in my life when everything was a challenge. We had just moved to Victoria, but my husband was working away and was only home a third of the time. I was left to move in, raise two teenagers, and cope with day-to-day life while struggling financially.

Looking back, I had yet to come to terms with the demons of my own childhood. It was a happy one, but one that left me with low self-esteem and striving for perfection in all aspects of my life.

Enter Deb! She was a ray of sunshine. That was my first impression. Little did I know that we were not unalike in our struggles but for very different reasons.

Beta Sigma Phi is a group of women coming together to support one another and have some fun. That is where we met. Deb put her heart and soul into everything she took on, and I often found myself admiring her endless energy and tenacity. She had the most beautiful smile and a raucous laugh that was utterly contagious.

When we moved off-island eight years later, I was unsure if our friendship would endure the separation, but magically, we came together once again for the Pursuit of Excellence in Vancouver, a program that changed both our lives. As participants, we learned how to set aside ineffective behaviours that got in the way of good relationships and so much more.

I don't care who you are, growing up is fraught with

landmines, big and small. Sometimes it only takes one comment from someone you love and trust to alter the way you see yourself and the world around you. My Dad was pivotal in my development. He was full of fun and loved us dearly, but I can still remember him saying two phrases that changed my perception of who I was: *Don't be so bloody stupid!* and *I thought you were smarter than that. Wow!* You have no idea how many times I incorporated those statements into my adult life. Only now, I was the one saying them.

What followed were years when Deb and I did not connect. Then, in 2015, a message turned up on my telephone. It was Deb asking to reconnect. It took another year before I drove up to her daughter's house to take her home overnight so that we could have a good visit. I was shocked when I saw her. She looked frail and had aged beyond her years. It wasn't until we were settled in front of the fireplace with a warm cup of tea that we started to catch up. It didn't take long before I realized that my long-lost friend was in trouble.

She told a story that gave me a clear understanding of just how ill she was. That was the bad news; the good news was that she was on a liver transplant list and was hoping to hear soon that they had found a match. Fear struck at my heart, and tears welled up as I listened to this beautiful woman who had become a shadow of her former self, and yet that beautiful smile and sense of resilience shone through.

I quickly agreed that if a transplant took place, she could count on me to provide support in Vancouver during her post-surgical recovery period, a requirement for any liver transplant recipient before receiving final approval.

Then, it happened. The phone rang, and I heard Deb say excitedly, *We are on the ferry to Vancouver; we got the call to get to the hospital!* We were all jumping for joy while at the same time hoping she would come through this very complicated surgery successfully.

Well, let's face it, Deb is a survivor, and her courage and resilience didn't let her down. Not only did she successfully get through one transplant, but when that one started to fail, a country-wide search for a second liver ended in a second one 25 days after the first.

Once recovery began, my stint as a caregiver kicked in. Those were precious days together, and predictably, not all easy. By that time, she had fewer physical needs, but we talked endlessly over that week, and I provided a good sounding board for her to voice the struggles she was facing, both emotionally and spiritually, now that she had a second chance at life.

You think you know someone well because you have spent hours talking about so many aspects of your lives, comparing experiences and being there for one another. And yet, I had barely touched the tip of the iceberg where Deb's life journey was concerned. I don't need to tell that story; Deb has done a beautiful job of doing that herself. In true *Deb fashion*, she has bared her soul with brutal honesty and gifted us with the opportunity to look within as we continue to move through the important lessons we choose to learn in this lifetime.

I truly believe each of us is on a journey, and every person we meet is meant to teach us something. Whether through the daily quotes Deb sends out to a large group of friends to provide encouragement and support, through our continuing interactions by phone and in person, or through this book, she will continue to be one of the important teachers in my life.

Gratitude is an important part of daily living, and I am thankful for so much. I feel that I have lived a blessed life, and

I know it is richer by far for having Deb in it. We will, the two of us, go to the end of our days knowing how deep and wide that friendship is.

Read on! As I did, you will undoubtedly recognize yourself somewhere in these pages, and you will come out stronger for it.

Thanks, Deb. It took courage to share your story with so much honesty. In the telling, you have given us all a precious gift.

Wendy Pratt
Former Executive Director
Nanaimo Community Hospice Society
Nanaimo, BC

Introduction

Thank you for picking up and reading my story. The environment I grew up in provided me with many opportunities to learn about myself, my surroundings, and what I wanted for my life and what I didn't. It was stable and nurturing on the one hand and unstable and chaotic on the other.

My story includes all the beautiful people who impacted my life in many ways and enabled me to find my voice, speak my truth, and trust myself.

The title of this book, *Evolving To Be Me: Kissing Death and Trusting Myself*, takes you on a journey of my life from childhood to the challenges of being a wife and mother and surviving two liver transplants.

My life has been an adventure with some ups and downs that helped me learn valuable lessons. I needed to learn to uncover the characteristics I developed as a child who grew up in an environment with a parent who had an alcohol addiction. I stood up for myself, felt and expressed my emotions, prioritized self-care, learned to trust myself and others, and created deep loving relationships.

I believe we are all given this one beautiful life, and it is up to us what we do with it. Little by little, in my early 20s, I began to shift my thinking and question my beliefs. I learned one of the ways I think is by using a recipe. I also realized I could choose to consider anything that happens in my life as a lesson, and I believe the lessons I learned helped me change my thought patterns and enabled me to become my authentic self.

In my early 20s, I purchased a fridge magnet that reads: *I like my bifocals; my dentures fit me fine; my hearing aid is perfect; but Lord, I miss my mind.* When I purchased it, I didn't quite picture myself wearing bifocals, dentures, or hearing aids. What I find particularly funny is the phrase, *Lord, I miss my mind.* As a young adult, I never forgot this phrase nor thought what a significant impact it would have on me. But it provided the awareness I needed to have a sincere appreciation for how important it is, and was, to take care of my mind.

Although this is not a recipe book, I have created and included one at the end of each chapter and a few recipes from others I picked up and used along the way. I hope that something I've experienced, learned, and shared on these pages is of value to you in some way. The recipes I included represent the lessons I learned and practiced that helped me to become my authentic self. I also shared a self-reflection and provided space for you, the reader, to create your recipes and self-reflection.

After my liver transplant, I thought I would write a memoir about my experience, hoping it would help others. It was challenging to put my story on paper because my inner critic kept telling me I was a terrible writer and reminded me of others who were better. I knew parts of my story were not unique. Many people share their fears of not being good enough or feeling unworthy. I know many people who have grown up in dysfunctional homes and believed it was my responsibility to inspire others to think they are enough, they are worthy, and that their past does not equal their future.

A friend invited me to a book launch for *Daring to Share Your Story: An Authentic Writing Guide* by Diana Reyers and

Tana Heminsley, which supports writing a memoir. Following the exercises and steps in this book helped me open up and be vulnerable and not shy away from my emotions and truths. It was the recipe I needed to finish writing my story.

I have loved quotes for many years, and this quote by Steve Jobs continues to have a positive impact on my life.

> *You can't connect the dots looking forward;*
> *you can only connect them looking backwards.*
> *So, you have to trust that the dots will somehow*
> *connect in your future.*

Everyone has their own story, journey, and lessons to learn. My intention in sharing my story is that you will see yourself somewhere on these pages and then write your recipe for your authentic life. I hope that my story resonates with and inspires you to embrace your worthiness and supports you to learn that you are enough and your past does not equal your future.

Each of us is enough, worthy, and we can speak our truth and be free to live authentically.

Evolving To Be Me

I

Going Back in Order to Move Forward

*In order to love who you are,
you cannot hate the experiences that shaped you.*

~ *Andrea Dykstra*

It's time for us to go home mom, my daughter said, *I have to go back to work tomorrow.* I struggled to open my eyes as I was disoriented and didn't understand. Hadn't they just got there? Why were they leaving so soon? It was then that I realized I had no recollection of the last five days.

In 1992, when I was 37, I was diagnosed with primary biliary cholangitis, I and was told I might need a liver transplant by the time I was 60. That day I opened my eyes was five days after my second liver transplant.

I know people who remember every important date in their life. But an important date to me may not be an important date to them. I remember my close family members' birthdays; however, I don't remember the exact date my dad passed away or the date I was diagnosed with PBC. I think my subconscious mind decides which dates are important to remember.

I remember dates that have significant meaning to me.

Evolving To Be Me

March 11, 2020, when the World Health Organization announced the world was in the throngs of a pandemic, will be one that I remember as the day the world, as I knew it, changed forever. Another date imprinted on my brain never to forget is July 11, 2016. It was the day I received my second liver transplant and a second chance at life.

> *Life is a journey, not a destination.*
>
> *~Ralph Waldo Emerson.*

Everyone's journey begins at birth, and their life unfolds from there. My parents, the environment I grew up in, the experiences that shaped my thoughts and beliefs, and the stories I heard and created along the way, influenced who I am today. Somewhere along my life's journey, I realized I needed to trust in something—my gut, destiny, life, karma, God, or the universe. This approach has never let me down, and it has made all the difference for me. I learned to trust each one of these at different times and sometimes all of them at once.

I believe we all have an underlying attitude or philosophy about life. Put another way, each of us sees the world differently. Pierre Teilhard de Chardin said,

> *We are not human beings having a spiritual experience.*
> *We are spiritual beings having a human experience.*

My philosophy is that I was given this beautiful gift called life, and at some point, I had to decide what to do with it. How I choose to see my circumstances from the past, for myself, and for going forward is a choice. I believe I survived my second liver transplant because I had been on a spiritual journey of

Chapter 1

self-discovery. I've learned that when I heal my mind by changing my thoughts, my mind can heal my body. This quote by Steve Jobs reiterates this belief,

> *You can't connect the dots looking forward,*
> *you can only connect them looking backwards.*
> *So, you have to trust that the dots will somehow*
> *connect in your future.*

Looking back, I know I may not have survived the second transplant that took place just 28 days after the first without the lifetime of influences I had: my parents, growing up when I did, meeting all the people I did, and experiencing everything I have—good and bad.

This memoir is a sharing of stories, outcomes, and life lessons, while introducing the people who influenced me along the way. My grandmother was a positive influence, and my happy place while growing up was spending many vacations on her farm in rural Saskatchewan. We had fun cooking, weeding her garden, going on picnics, driving down many worn dirt country roads, and listening to the grasshoppers while visiting some of my other relatives. During one of my visits when I was about six years old, I remember she was making cookies, and she helped me up on a stool, gave me a spoon, and showed me how to scoop out the dough onto a cookie sheet. I was so excited and happy, and from that day forward, I loved helping in the kitchen. My grandmother taught me how to bake, so I could create cookies and cakes by the age of ten. Since then and throughout adulthood, I've had lots of fun experimenting with baking and eventually took my skills to a higher level, expanding my list of recipes. Over time, I realized that perhaps there was an analogy between recipes for baking and a recipe for life. So, I had to ask myself, *What was my recipe for life?*

Looking back, I now realize, having a recipe gave me more confidence or a set of clear instructions for everything I approached in life. This way, I could be assured that the outcome could be positive; I thought there might be less chance of doing it wrong. And yet, even then, things didn't always turn out as planned, and I found myself feeling very frustrated. Eventually, I began to realize that a recipe was only a guideline, a place to start to see what worked and what didn't. Just as in life, some recipes have more than one ingredient and different directions. Thus, over the years, I became open to trying different approaches to relationships, careers, and even how and where I live.

Based on Pierre Teilhard de Chardin's quote about spiritual beings having a human experience, the recipe analogy makes sense to me. Here I am a spiritual being in this world, trying to find the right recipe or approach, and it's usually just trial and error. Many times, when things didn't turn out, I got upset and threw my hands up in the air. Usually, my frustration was followed by a strong desire to run and hide, but eventually, I found I could just tweak the recipe and try something different.

I created a few recipes that have worked for me throughout my life, as well as a few I've received from others. One of them that helped my husband and me came in a poster we received from my sister entitled, *Rules for a Happy Marriage*. As a young married couple, it gave us a place to start. In each case, whether the approach I formulated was a success or not, it supported me to find my voice at a time when I realized I didn't have one. I wasn't sure how that happened, where it went, or why I could not express myself. So, I began to examine my life more closely and realized that many circumstances from my childhood

Chapter 1

shaped who I was. This quest for self-awareness has taken me from feeling deep shame to life-affirming pride within how I live today.

When I first started writing my memoir, I had an overwhelming sense of not knowing where to start. As I shared my feelings with my soul mate, my life partner, I began to realize I was extremely hesitant to write about my childhood. I did not want to go back and relive the pain, the feelings of unworthiness, and the shame that came with them. I thought I had spent my whole life healing my body, mind, and spirit from the environment I grew up in. Of course, all childhood circumstances are relative, but I came to understand that some of mine left me with many insecurities, a negative outlook on life, and the feeling of not being good enough. Sometimes, I just wished I could disappear but realized I needed to understand where my negative stories, thoughts, beliefs, and unworthiness came from in order to be proud of who I have become.

I knew I was an adult child of an alcoholic father and decided to educate myself on some of the characteristics and personality traits I had developed as a result. In her 1983 landmark book, *Adult Children of Alcoholics*, the late Janet G. Woititz, Ed.D, outlined 13 characteristics and personality traits associated with children raised by alcoholics.[1]

Adult children of alcoholics (ACoAs) often:

- Guess at what normal behavior is.
- Have difficulty following a project through from beginning to end.
- Lie when it would be just as easy to tell the truth.

---

[1] Janet G. Woititz ED. D., Adult Children of Alcoholics, Health Communications Inc., 1983

- Judge themselves without mercy.
- Have difficulty having fun.
- Take themselves very seriously.
- Have difficulty with intimate relationships.
- Overreact to changes over which they have no control.
- Constantly seek approval and affirmation.
- Feel that they're different from other people.
- Are super responsible or super irresponsible.
- Are extremely loyal, even in the face of evidence that the loyalty is undeserved.
- Are impulsive.
- People may tend to lock themselves in a course of action without giving serious consideration to alternative behaviors or possible consequences.
- A person's impulsively can lead to confusion, self-loathing, and loss of control over their environment. In addition, the person spends an excessive amount of energy cleaning up the mess.

I've learned that not all the characteristics may apply to me. However, reviewing this list helped me identify the ones I developed to survive in a dysfunctional environment. As I began writing about my background, stories, thoughts, and beliefs, I resonated with many of the characteristics listed above, which helped me to understand why I thought the way I thought and where my beliefs and stories came from.

I recognized that many occurrences growing up left me feeling like I couldn't be me or express myself effectively. One of the phrases my dad used to say was, *Children are to be seen and not heard.* I'm sure he heard this from his parents or someone else close to him. I didn't realize I perceived I was abandoned by my dad as a child. But then, some years ago, my

Chapter 1

mom told me that when he was supposed to be looking after me, I was left alone on the couch in our trailer looking out the window, waiting for my mom to come home from work. I was around two at the time and have no doubt he was invited to a bar for a drink, and I was in the way of that. I'm certain this incident influenced my ability to form a trusting bond with my dad.

We lived in a two-room shack in a small town in Saskatchewan when I was about five years old. One day, a friend and I wandered off to explore the town and lost track of the time. We found a swing set in a back yard and were transformed into a dream world of imagination. Little did I know my grandfather was taken to the hospital in another town, and my dad and a visiting uncle were frustrated that they had to scour the streets, looking for me. When I wandered through the door without a care in the world, my dad released his frustration and anger onto me. I was terrified and ended up getting the spanking of my life. My inner child shook with fear and hid, never to come out until years later. Looking back on this traumatic event, I know it caused some emotional damage, linking being carefree and having fun with fear and disappointment. From that day forward, I was frightened and anxious whenever my dad was around.

At the time, I thought it was my fault my grandfather was in the hospital and that being a free spirit and experiencing joy was not okay. Moving forward, I tried very hard not to be me, but rather what others wanted me to be. I found myself repeatedly trying to conform, to fit in instead of standing out. Whenever any kind of confrontation happened at school, at home, or with friends, I distinguished my mind and body wanting to contort. Some of my thoughts were: *You should have done this, you should have said that, you should have stayed home, you should have worn something else.* I escaped from my real life for days, maybe weeks, trying to be different, think different, do things differently. Eventually, with only the resilience that a child can find, I finally discovered the courage to be myself again. Then Bam! Something happened, and I headed down the slippery slope of beating myself up, turning myself upside down and inside out. I was well into my fifties before I recognized this pattern of behaviour, and when these thoughts and feelings came up, I was finally able to say, *Just STOP!*

When I was 17 years old one of my cousins, who was 22 and had a young child, died suddenly from an epileptic seizure at home. I was out having fun with my friends, and when I got home, these were the words my dad said to me, *We couldn't find you, and your cousin died.* It was like my 17-year-old mind and emotions were catapulted back 12 years to the scene in Saskatchewan when my dad released all his frustration and anger on me. Feeling like it was my fault and that being free and having fun was not okay came flooding back. I developed a sense that when an adverse incident occurred in my family, it was my fault if I wasn't home.

My home-life was chaotic, and I was always uneasy and assumed I was powerless. I was the oldest and, I was taught that the oldest is supposed to set an example for their siblings. However, every fiber of my being was filled with self-loathing, shame, and unworthiness. I now realize that these underlying feelings shaped my adult life. However, they also eventually gave me the opportunity to find my voice and to start standing up for myself.

In hindsight, I know that my dad severely lacked self-esteem and was unable to express himself and label his emotions. It was really challenging for me because I was afraid to do or say anything around him for fear it might be wrong, and I might

Chapter 1

hear about it later. I walked around on eggshells, with my spirit being crushed from one moment to the next; I often just wanted to disappear. The confusing thing was that when he was sober, he was a very mild mannered, gentle kind of guy. When an incident occurred that he didn't like, he said nothing about it most of the time. But then, over the next few days or weeks, when he came home drunk, he might bring up the incident in a rage. Many times, I didn't even remember what he was upset about, but I never forgot how I perceived myself around him—distant and frightened.

What I do remember was being left with the feeling of not being good enough and not being worthy of praise, acknowledgement, or acceptance. I was an energetic child and craved being free and adventurous. I was curious about everything, and I wanted to explore the world around me, and make friends with the children in my neighborhood. But I perceived my home as a dark, unsafe place, and I feared doing or saying anything, and especially being who I really was.

I worked tirelessly to be a good daughter and support to my mother, as well as a good sister and granddaughter. My father was absent a lot of the time, either out of town working, at the bar, or glued to the TV, watching the latest sports event when he was home. It didn't seem to matter how hard I worked or how much I did. I continuously sought his approval, yet every time he drank, he said things like: *Who do you think you are? Lady Godiva!* Later, I recognized that the most challenging thing for me to do is relax, slow down, and be. It's like I've had my dad sitting on my shoulders repeating this in my ear for years. I now know that this is an old tape, a developed thought, and a made-up story, but when I was growing up and heard him say this, I envisioned a woman lying on a chaise lounge with servants surrounding her. They were fanning her and feeding her grapes. I heard what he said in a negative context and assumed she and I were lazy slobs. Recently, I decided to do some research to find out who this Lady Godiva was. It turns out, she was popularized in a 900-year-old English legend as an 11th century noblewoman who was determined to help the public; she was known for her generosity to the church. It turns out the story I told myself was incorrect, but from my perspective my dad's message was clear—I was a lazy slob!

As an adult, I suffered from believing I was unworthy. While writing and doing research, I learned that my lack of worthiness was developed in my childhood. It became clear that my alcoholic dad projected his sense of inadequacy onto me. He often said, *Why bother, you aren't going to amount to anything anyway.* Although my mom was an enabler, I am certain she was unaware that she was. She did not have the ability to express her emotions to my dad. I'm pretty sure she did not know how to set boundaries and was afraid that if she made any changes, her situation could get worse. What I heard from my dad and what was reiterated by my mom not defending me was that I was not gifted in any way or good at anything. Since my thoughts, beliefs, and sense of self confirmed this, it transferred outside my home to my school and during interactions with others. Naturally, I believed for years that I was not worthy. How could I not?

As a child, I believed I fell short in most aspects of my life. I wasn't an A student or an athlete. In my mind, I simply didn't measure up. Dad used to say, *Why can't you be like so and so?* As an adult. I constantly compared myself and my accomplishments to others; in my mind, I usually fell short. I finally asked myself, *When will it be time to let go of these stories? When can I lay them down and tell them to take a seat? Am I still trying to earn my dad's appreciation or praise?* It was crazy making since my dad had

Chapter 1

passed away many years ago. This was an old story, and it was time to write a new one.

My research revealed that some parents in dysfunctional families blame or project their negative emotions onto their children. My dad learned to dislike himself and to judge himself as being unworthy and projected the same onto me. I took on the emotional baggage my family transferred onto me, and as a result, I constantly thought I should be doing more to fix it. But the messages I received were wrong, and it was not my fault. I lived through a distorted reality that I bought into to survive in a dysfunctional environment. Today I know in my heart that this is not my stuff to carry!

I ended up coming back to doing the research that always served me well and decided to look up the definition of worthiness to learn what ingredients support self-worth. My research includes the definition of worthy and an excerpt from a Psychology Today article, *What Makes A Person Worthy? 'The Four Bs.'*[2]

Worthy Definition[3]
adjective, **wor·thi·er, wor·thi·est.**

1. having adequate or great merit, character, or value: *a worthy successor.*

2. of commendable excellence or merit; deserving: *a book worthy of praise; a person worthy to lead.*
3. *noun, plural* **wor·thies.**

---

[2] Saul Levine, M.D., What Makes A Worthy Person? "The 4 B's", Psychology Today, March 8, 2016
[3] https://www.dictionary.com/browse/worthy

a person of eminent worth, merit, or position: *The town worthies included two doctors.*

What Makes a Person Feel Worthy? 'The Four Bs'

The genuine appreciation of our worthiness and quality depends on our achieving the state of what I call The Four Bs: Being, Belonging, Believing, and Benevolence.

Being *(Personal): People with a sense of Being have a sense of inner peace and self-acceptance and feel grounded and at ease. They are grateful for who they have become and how they've acted with others. They have a realistic self-image in that they're aware of their faults and limitations. They appreciate themselves despite their mistakes, imperfections, and yes, physical, and emotional scars. They've been caring and generous to others and have redeemed and forgiven themselves.*

Belonging *(Social): People with a sense of Belonging are members of at least one group or community that is important to them, where they feel liked and appreciated, and they reciprocate those feelings. This could be a family, a congregation, club, gang, team, platoon, or other community. Members feel an organic affiliation and comfort with others who share values and traditions and provide support, respect, and friendship. These relationships prevent the anxieties of loneliness, provide pleasure, and enhance life. The warm glow of belonging contributes to physical and emotional health, and quality of life.*

Believing *(Ethical/Spiritual): A sense of believing refers to guiding values and ethics of behaviour. Millions of people venerate* *a God who gives them comfort and hope and provides a set of moral rules for their conduct. But one need not believe in a Supreme Being to be ethical. Religious followers are no more principled or compassionate than agnostics and atheists. What is critically important to human beings is their need to believe in a system of moral principles and civil behaviour. When we adhere to principles based on religion, or humanism, or other humane social philosophy, our lives are more meaningful, in times of joy as well as pain. When we humans wonder about issues beyond everyday materialism and are in awe about how minuscule we are in the millions of universes, we are removed from the fray and transported to a spiritual realm.*

Benevolence: *A sense of benevolence is an awareness of how kind and generous we have been or the positive effects we have had on others. Benevolence is a culmination of the other Bs. Our personal legacies are best represented by our acts of decency and caring for each other. Notwithstanding our history of aggression and violence, we humans are genetically predisposed to be helpful to others in need. We can also learn to behave with more tolerance and generosity. The kindness and goodness we bestow on others throughout our lives is the essence of a sense of benevolence.*

The Four Bs are essential to all who are honestly evaluating the worth of their lives. They are the foundation for our core legacies, which means "Our Emotional Footprint."

After reading the definitions and learning about the four Bs, I recognized that I am, in fact, worthy. I also discovered my developed mindset of unworthiness because I grew up in a dysfunctional environment. I also knew, of course, that I was not the only one. I have decided to rewrite my life story because I know I am enough, I do enough, and I am worthy. Following is how I describe my 'Four Bs:'

Being: *I do my best to be present within my day-to-day life: my emotions, my feelings, and those I am interacting with. What am I worthy of? I am worthy of being at peace with myself as I feel grounded and proud of how I treat others. I accept myself for who I am, scars and all—both physical and emotional. I forgive myself and others for not being perfect and accept that we are all human.*

Belonging: *I know I belong to my family, my friends, and my community. I volunteer to support seniors to feel seen and heard as we all navigate our ever-changing world. I support many groups of friends by listening and showing compassion and empathy for where they are on their journey. I know I matter to many family members, friends, and my community which contributes to my physical and mental health, and overall quality of life.*

Believing: *I believe strongly in a higher power—the "Universe." Creating a connection with something greater than myself helps me feel the essence of a sense of benevolence. I have hope for the future of humanity. I see the spirit that sustains each of us every day.*

Benevolence: *Over the years, I have developed the capacity to be kind, caring, generous, and empathetic towards others. I demonstrate these characteristics by taking the time to be present, listening to understand, and putting myself in another's shoes. I know I have a positive effect on those I interact with.*

Growing up I had no idea I was developing an unworthy mindset. Living with a father who had an addiction created a dysfunctional home, and for me, that meant it wasn't safe

Chapter 1

to speak my truth. This included not revealing truths about my family, gossiping amongst family members, and learning enabling patterns of familial behaviour to excuse, justify, ignore, deny, and cope with my family environment.

I was not aware of why I was anxious and concluded that I had to organize my behavior around my dad's needs and choices. Our entire family enabled him by always fixing, solving, or making the consequences of his behaviour go away. Although we perceived we were being manipulated and held like emotional hostages, we continued this behaviour pattern because we knew my dad relied on his family, and we were desperate to prevent an enormous, pending, unknown crisis.

I first became aware I started finding my voice and changing my behavior after I got married and moved to another city. My husband and I went to visit my family one weekend, and my dad and I were sitting on the couch. He started complaining about one of my siblings and said they were ripping him off. I sat there not saying a word, which surprised him, so he reacted by saying, *Has the cat got your tongue?* I replied, *What do you expect me to say? If you have an issue, you need to discuss it with them.* Where did the courage to say that come from, I wondered? We were both a bit surprised at my reaction, but I had grown up, matured, and was learning to no longer participate in family gossip—at least, not with my dad. It took me much longer to change this pattern with my siblings.

About twelve years after my husband and I were married, my family members were encouraged to do an intervention with my dad. The purpose of the intervention was to inform my dad he had a drinking problem and for our family to learn how to set boundaries around his behaviour that affected us negatively. We lived several hours away, and when my family asked for our support, all the old feelings of abandonment and disappointment came flooding back. My first reaction was that I had life challenges and fish to fry, so to speak. I just wanted to ignore their request since my dad didn't usually keep his commitments. In the end, I still knew I needed to support my mom and my siblings, so my husband and I did what it took to attend the intervention. The meeting was scheduled around us because we were travelling from out of the province and had to take time off work. The intention was that each person share their concern for his health and let him know how his behaviour impacted their lives. Each of us were to set boundaries regarding how we wanted to be treated and what behavior we expected from him going forward.

I was disappointed and very frustrated because my husband and I moved heaven and earth to attend the intervention, and once again, dad didn't have the decency to show up. My family rescheduled the intervention for about a month later and somehow got my dad there. However, we were unable to attend. To support my family, I agreed to speak with my dad to communicate my concerns and boundaries going forward if he drank. Several months after the intervention, he came to visit me and said he was never going to stop drinking. He shared that I was the only one in the family he could be himself with. The only thing I thought of saying was, *Perhaps your comfort with me comes from the fact that we do not interact on a day-to-day basis.* I came to realize that he thought our relationship was just fine, and maybe for him it was. I knew it was a different dynamic for my mom and siblings, and I observed my feelings of guilt and shame.

When I got a little older, I noticed very few aunts, uncles, or cousins came to visit. My Mom sometimes told us about relatives from out of town who came to visit my dad's sister but didn't come to see us. I never really understood the situation,

Chapter 1

and when I was in my early teens, I asked my mom why they never came to visit us. She answered by relaying an old family joke directed at my dad when he was growing up and carried over into his adulthood. It seemed no one knew where it came from or had the communication skills to address it, and my dad did not have the self-esteem or courage to put a stop to it. I can only imagine how this one joke must have shaped him psychologically from the day it was told to the day he died.

Once again, I turned to researching how siblings impact one another and learned they can have a profound lingering effect on the human psyche. What I learned in my dad's case was that his siblings had a significant negative influence on him. Although the term sibling bullying may not have been around in the early 40s and 50s, this incident could be considered a form of bullying by today's standards. In my dad's family dynamics, their sibling conflict increased from childhood into adulthood.

I do not know whether my nanny, who was my dad's mom, played a role in him being the brunt of a family joke or not. Perhaps she was unaware of what took place amongst her children. But from what I can gather, dad's siblings teased him incessantly from a very young age about the fact that he was John Jones' kid. My understanding of John Jones was that he was a neighbor. This situation might be like a mother telling her child he was the milkman's child, with resulting feelings of being ostracised from your family. Psychologically, this is a big deal because achieving a sense of belonging is a fundamental psychological need. Being mocked and rejected time and time again by his siblings likely had an impact on my dad's self-esteem and any sense of control and meaningful connection with his family.

There was a lot I didn't know about my dad's upbringing,

17

but I quickly realized it might behoove me to learn as much as I could. The little knowledge I acquired has helped me understand who he was, and how his background, thoughts, and beliefs likely impacted and shaped who he was. And ultimately, this shaped me.

When my dad was 61, he was diagnosed with lung cancer and given two months to live. My family and I were living in another province when I heard the news, and I became anxious, concerned I wouldn't see him before he passed away. I am eternally grateful he lived another three years, and I got the chance to say good-bye. It was the summer of 1992 when I sensed this might be the last opportunity that I had to make peace with him before he died; I knew I didn't want to have any regrets. I was reading all kinds of books at the time and got my hands on a one by Dr. David Stoop entitled, *Making Peace with Your Father*. I knew I wanted to heal our relationship and share the positive influences he had on my life with him.

In my heart of hearts, I knew I needed to muster up a lot of courage to talk to my dad one-on-one, and I had no idea what I was going to say. So, I brought along the book, thinking I could somehow read it and get advice before I saw him. Both my husband's family and mine lived in various parts of Alberta, so any time we went to visit, it was a whirlwind of house-hopping to fit everyone in. We were only in Edmonton for a few days, and I put pressure on myself to spend time with my sisters, my brother, and my mother, as well as make time to see my dad on his own.

I was staying at my sisters, and because I wasn't good at setting boundaries or communicating my needs, I was up into the wee hours of the morning speed reading the most relevant chapters of the book. I asked my sister to look after my children for a few hours; they were nine and eleven at the time. When

Chapter 1

I went to make the phone call to set up a time to see my dad face-to-face, I was an emotional wreck. This was something I had never done before, and I had no idea what the outcome might be.

Amazingly, I was able to share some of my most cherished memories of the qualities I admired the most about him, as well as the positive influence he had on my life. My dad had the best belly laugh, the most beautiful smile, and a kind heart. That day, he told me that he never meant to hurt the people in his life. We spent that summer afternoon talking about old times, laughing at our family dynamics, appreciating one another and the positive parts of the relationship we had. I look back on that day with deep gratitude knowing it was worth the effort it took to make it happen. My sister came to pick me up, and as we drove away from the house, I turned to see my dad standing on the porch with the sun beaming down on him as he grinned from ear-to-ear and waved goodbye.

I got the midnight phone call in January 1994 that he passed away in his sleep at home. I flew to Edmonton with my husband and children for his funeral, and for their own reasons, my family in Edmonton wanted an open casket. The last memory I wanted to hold in my heart was of him standing on the porch grinning from ear to ear and waving goodbye, not seeing him lying in a coffin. I thought my family needed my support, and I didn't want to create a confrontation especially at my dad's funeral. I entered that room for all of two minutes and told them, *I'm sorry I can't stay here.* It was difficult for me to leave the room because it seemed like I was abandoning my family at a time when they really needed my support.

Although I strengthened my relationship with my dad before he passed away, there were many times I continued to hear his voice. One such time was when I was in my fifties and was off work for about two weeks because I had contracted shingles. My doctor insisted I stay home for another week, and I was distraught about having to call my boss; I had never missed three weeks of work. I sat in my vehicle after my appointment, and all I could do was cry. I wondered, *Why am I crying?* I sat there for a few minutes and heard my dad's voice loud and clear, *What good are you if you can't work?* Oh my God, that old record was still playing in my head! Once I realized this, I calmed down and was able to telephone my boss without feeling guilty.

Another time in my late fifties, my husband and I had some good friends over for dinner, and we were discussing when I needed to leave work due to my failing liver. During the conversation, I realized my definition of sick came from my dad, and that I held the belief that if I wasn't on death's door, I had no excuse—I wasn't sick enough to take time off. Once again, I heard my dad's voice as if he was standing in front of me, *You're not sick enough to stay home from school.* As I shared this belief out loud to my friends, I realized it was not serving me anymore, and it was up to me to do something about it. This conversation helped me to re-evaluate my definition of sick and recognize it was time to take the necessary steps to ask about applying for long-term disability.

I know I wouldn't be the person I am today without having the dad I had. I learned a lot from him, and I believe I created a clear mental picture of what I did not want my life to look like. Over time, I learned how to visualize myself as a happily married woman, who cared deeply for her family, so I took the time to learn how to be a better person, partner, mother and to further find my voice. I thought, *What else is more important than that?*

Chapter 1

My Recipe for Moving Forward

- *Awareness is the first step to change;*
- *To move forward in life, go back;*
- *Learn what I don't want from those I love;*
- *Do my homework, research, ask questions, then take action;*
- *Write a new recipe when I presume I am unworthy;*
- *Learn from past exposures; know that the past does not equal the future;*
- *Do better to know better;*
- *Life is a journey, not a destination.*

My Self-Reflection

My parents and other adults influenced and shaped my life in one way or another. They may not have been the best role models, but in some ways, maybe they were. I now believe both my dad and mom did the best they could. What I recognized was that this is my life, and it's up to me to learn from my past, heal my thoughts and beliefs, and change my stories. Over time, I learned that when I choose positive empowering thoughts and change some of the beliefs that are no longer serving me, I can create a happy fulfilling life.

What is Your Recipe for Moving Forward?

Chapter 1

Given Your Recipe, Share Your Self-Reflection

II

Childhood Experiences Can Be A Blessing

The highest form of ignorance is when you reject something you don't know anything about.

~ Wayne Dyer

When I was a child, my family moved around a lot, never living in one province or place for more than a year or two, so I assumed I didn't make friends easily because we moved so much. However, years later, my mom said that I didn't keep friends easily because she told their mothers I had celiac and not to feed me.

One of the first places I lived in was a trailer. It was on a farm where my mom was the housekeeper and cook. I remember running through the cow pasture because I loved the warm rays of the sun on my face and the free-flowing breeze blowing through my hair. Oops, sometimes I wasn't paying attention and stepped in a cow patty. Yuck!

I was four years old when my sister was born. My mom tells me that I thought my sister was a gift for me because I played with her as if she was my favourite doll. I recall one fierce winter, with so much snow that it reached the top of the door frame when my dad went outside. He had to dig through the snow with a shovel. Since my dad often worked out of town, we were particularly grateful he was home to do the digging.

When we moved to Edmonton, Alberta, my parents rented a half-duplex, which was nicer than most houses we lived in. Shortly after my brother was born, my mom started to babysit for other parents. I was seven, and a memory that stands out for me was a five-year-old boy who arrived around seven in the morning and run down the hallway pretending to ride his horse and sing at the top of his lungs *dunt ta dunt ta da da ta da*, the opening song to the TV show Bonanza. I'm pretty sure he woke up our family, along with the neighbours on the other side of the duplex. From then on, mornings weren't my best time of the day while growing up.

During that time, I made a friend and was invited to her house to play after school. This was one of my first invitations to someone else's place, and I didn't know what to expect. It didn't take long for me to notice that her mother seemed to always be in her bedroom. I thought this was odd because I only saw my mom in bed at night. After several months, my friend told me that her mom had died. I was so sad for my friend and wanted to be there for her to help somehow, but we moved shortly after that. I remember thinking that I couldn't imagine losing my mom, and I tried to put myself in her place—lost, alone, and scared. Experiencing this through the eyes of a child changed my life forever. It taught me not to take my mom for granted and to appreciate all she did for me. I am very blessed that she is still alive, and we have a warm and close relationship that I cherish to this day.

Somewhere along the way, I learned that my mom lost two children before I was born. She married my dad when she was 20 and had my brother six months later in October of 1953. He

Chapter 2

died seven weeks later, and no one seemed to know why. My sister was born a year later in November of 1954 and died in my mother's arms a year after that. My mom was alone when her daughter died, and she told me years later she took a cab to the hospital. The doctors told my mom that she died from complications of cystic fibrosis. I cannot fathom the grief she endured, being on her own with my dad unavailable and no other family member to support her. I came along one month after my sister died, so she hardly had time to grieve before she found herself caring for a new baby. She and my dad did not ever speak about these profound losses. Like many men of that era, my father had a very hard time with grief and emotions, and he turned to alcohol to ease his pain.

Although my dad was often out of town working, I'm not sure he provided his family with steady financial support. My mom was often on her own and was more or less a single mother with four children to raise, including me. Although she was swamped most of the time, taking care of her kids, working, and keeping up with the never-ending household chores, she always had time to listen. My father was more like a fifth child for her than a partner, supportive father, or husband. I took on the role of a co-parent, being my mom's right-hand man. I was always very close to my siblings since I looked after them from a very young age. I'm so grateful for them and hold a great deal of love, compassion, and empathy for all my family members.

Several very traumatic events took place when I was ten and eleven years old during the school year. Until recently, I did not realize they all happened within a short time. The first took place when my mom contracted Hepatitis E. She was extremely ill and couldn't get out of bed for ten days. I had to stay home from school to look after my three siblings. When

I returned to school, I was overwhelmed, sinking in the belief that I couldn't catch up because I was so far behind.

A few months later, the second incident occurred one night when my mom asked my seven-year-old sister to bring a shovel in from the front yard. It was the middle of winter, and when she didn't return, we thought she must have been abducted. The police came to our home and took me to our friends and neighbors to ask if anyone had seen my sister. I recall being frightened and helpless and remember being furious with my dad for not being there, for leaving mom, once again, to handle a situation on her own. Much to everyone's relief, my sister was returned home around 11 in the evening, with the police coming back to talk to her, and I was so relieved and grateful. Like most situations, while growing up, our family never talked about what really happened.

After reflecting on this incident, I realized that I took on a lot of the blame, thinking *I should have protected my sister; I should have got the shovel myself; I should, I should, I should!* Over time, I learned that I had to tell myself, Let it go; It was not my fault; I always did enough and was enough. However, even many years later, it's still hard to process.

The third and most stressful incident encompassed several events that occurred about four months later when my mom and dad decided to split up. My grandmother suggested we rent a house in a small town in Saskatchewan to be closer to her. The house was on the *wrong side of the tracks*, and I was the city kid starting grade six in the middle of the school year. I found school very challenging. I had no friends, and I was bullied and ridiculed. I was always the last one picked for sports events and school projects. What helped me get through my shame and manage my insecurities was living closer to my grandmother and being focused on supporting my mom and a few neighbours.

Chapter 2

To help with expenses, my mom asked her brother to live with us. He had schizophrenia and worked as a hired hand on a farm where he was responsible for moving the irrigation equipment from one plot of land to another. My uncle stayed in a small trailer while working the night shift. One evening, he asked my mom if he was allowed to take me with him. I don't think either one of us thought I was in danger. In fact, I was very excited and thought it might be a great adventure. I was extremely blessed as a young girl that I was able to recognize when something didn't seem right. The trailer had bunk beds, and he suggested I get into bed and cuddle with him, which I did. However, when he started to fondle my private parts, I knew something was wrong and crawled out of the lower bunk and moved into the top one. Fortunately for me, he was not a violent man and left me alone. I'm not sure if I told my mom what happened back then, but I told her I didn't want to go to work with my uncle again. The next time he asked her, she said no.

A few months after the incident with my uncle, my parents decided to get back together. My mom left my siblings and me with my grandmother on her farm while she travelled to help my dad prepare to move the family back to Edmonton. One day, my grandmother took my youngest sister and brother out to the bunkhouse to have a nap; it was a small building converted from a chicken coup to a bedroom with two separate beds. My grandfather, who was much older than my grandmother, also took a nap. Since we had just had lunch, my sister and I decided to help out by doing the dishes. It was 1965, and the farm was in rural Saskatchewan with no running water and an outhouse as a bathroom. Our first step was to boil the dishwater on an old wood stove—no small feat for a seven and eleven-year-old. The stove was hot enough from lunch to boil the water, and we gathered all the dishes and put them in the dish pan. I carried the boiling kettle to the counter, but it was very heavy, so when I went to set it down, it tipped, and the boiling water went all over the kitchen floor.

My grandmother was a very busy farmer's wife who worked extremely hard and didn't have time for accidents. She was also very kind, making us treats, taking us on picnics, and accompanying us to visit our other relatives. However, she could easily flip her lid if there was a big mess to clean up. My little sister had bare feet and hopped up and down, trying to stay away from the boiling water. We grabbed some towels and tried to clean up the mess. At this point, I was completely stressed and overwhelmed and made sure my grandfather was still sleeping, but he was sitting on the edge of the bed. Then, I went to see if my grandmother was still in the bunkhouse, but I saw she was headed straight for the house. The world was closing in on me, and all I wanted to do was explain what happened to prevent her from getting angry. I opened the front door and took several steps before blacking out. The world stopped, and all I can remember saying repeatedly was, *Will I ever see my Mommy again.*

Apparently, the stress was too much for my eleven-year-old brain to handle, and I fell to the ground, eating the dirt. My grandmother acted quickly and likely saved my life. She had my sister stick a spoon in my mouth and hold it there while she drove to the hospital. The doctors told my grandmother that I had a grand mal seizure, and I was diagnosed with epilepsy. After that, I took medication off and on until I was about 21, when I asked my doctor for an EEG to determine if I did, in fact, have epilepsy or if my seizure was a one-off due to stress. They could not detect any sign of the disease, and I've been off medication and seizure-free ever

Chapter 2

since. Since that time, I also learned that celiac disease could cause epilepsy in children.

We moved back to Edmonton, and life carried on pretty much the same. Although I was a very energetic child, I wasn't always healthy. While growing up, after I ate something, I felt sick. In fact, food and I were not friends; I disliked it and thought it disliked me! I remember my mom telling me I was celiac. *What the heck did that mean?* I had no idea. Since my parents had lost two children, the doctors decided to do some tests on me when I was born. They confirmed I was celiac and recommended I remain on a very strict diet for the rest of my life. I can only imagine how overwhelmed my mom must have been with yet another vulnerable child to care for.

I knew my mom ensured I followed a strict gluten-free diet until I was four years old. Once my sister was born, and two other siblings followed, I believe it was financially impossible to continue. This was the 50s, 60s and 70s, so there was not the abundance of gluten-free food items there is today, and what was available was expensive. How many families back then didn't eat Kraft Dinner, peanut butter and jam, bologna sandwiches, canned tomato soup, or grilled cheese sandwiches for lunch or dinner, and pancakes or cold cereal for breakfast. These foods were part of our weekly diet because they were inexpensive but not at all gluten-free.

I was always a skinny child, and because I didn't like eating, I often skipped meals or forgot to eat. Since I didn't understand what celiac was, any food I did eat was mostly bad for me, and I think I was so used to feeling sick after I ate certain things that I thought it was normal. My mom was very concerned about my health and prepared eggnogs in the morning, which were gluten-free, so I had something on my stomach for school.

For some reason, I thought that since I was diagnosed with

a disease, I should be sicker than I was. Back then, there was no internet, and as a kid, I never even thought to ask my doctor what celiac was. My mom is one of the most patient people I know; she is kind and compassionate and always has been. I always tried to help her. I would bake, cook, care for children, and do household chores, which in my mind, reaffirmed my value and usefulness. I recall always feeling safe and relieved when my mom was home, and even when she wasn't, I knew she was only a phone call away.

I didn't get good grades in school, and I wasn't athletic. Struggling to fit in, along with poor self-esteem, I had a hard time trusting myself and others, with no idea how to have fun. Then, in my junior high year, a physical education teacher recognized that I could run and suggested I train for a half-mile race. I competed at the district level and achieved a yellow ribbon, coming in fourth. Receiving the ribbon was a BIG deal because the first and second place winners were two other girls from my class. That precious ribbon was one of the only forms of recognition I ever received in school. It was also the first time I became aware of the difference between being proud and feeling shame.

When I was 13, Mom cleaned offices in the evening to support her family. She worked from five to ten in the evening and had to take an hour-long bus ride downtown to be at work on time. This meant I had to come home right after school, and there were times I was resentful because I couldn't go to a friend's house to play. I looked after my sister who was nine, my brother, seven, and my youngest sister, five, while Mom worked. I made sure they had supper and then put them to bed.

One evening, I was out in the backyard with my brother and youngest sister when I heard a bloodcurdling scream coming from inside the house. My mind was racing, and my heart was

Chapter 2

pounding—*what catastrophe did I have to handle now?* My nine-year-old sister used the bathroom and went to our bedroom window to look out at us in the backyard. While doing so, she accidentally hit her forehead on the open window, and it came crashing down on her finger. I ran into the house to find blood dripping all over the floor and her finger hanging from a thread. I am grateful I have always been level-headed and calm in times of crisis. It was fortunate that a neighbourhood kid was playing in our backyard, so I immediately directed her to get her mom to take my sister to the hospital. I stayed home with my brother and youngest sister. As I recall these memories, I recognize the tremendous pressure I must have been under, and I am so much more aware of why I was somewhat challenged in school. I likely didn't have time for homework and was very tired since I stayed up until my mom got home from work.

I judged my dad for not being there for his family. I also blamed him for the stressful situations I found myself in. I thought that if he worked close to home and didn't need to travel, my mom wouldn't have to work at night. Then, perhaps I wouldn't need to be the co-parent I was. As a result of his absences, I took on a great deal of responsibility for the well-being of my family. That meant I also believed that everything that happened to my family was my fault, and I needed to fix it all.

I hid my shame and that of my family by helping others. I babysat and always tried to support others. My mom was always volunteering for some organization or another, and I often went with her. Sometimes, we did dishes at a church after an afternoon tea, while other times, we went door to door collecting donations for one organization or another. I loved the praise, recognition, and acceptance I received from the adults at these events, providing a sense of being important and special. In addition, I loved experiencing the variety, adventure, and feelings of accomplishment that came along with helping others. I'm grateful my mom introduced me to volunteering because it gave me an opportunity to be proud of myself and learn many skills while helping others.

My Mom tried to seek counselling several times and learned about the organization Al-Anon, a support group for families affected by alcoholism. She went to several meetings, but I believe she was overwhelmed by the effort it took to ride a bus there and back, in addition to the responsibilities she already had on her plate. She learned that they also had a support group for teens called Alateen and suggested I attend a meeting. I remember going to several meetings and being angry and bewildered that I had to spend my evenings riding a bus and then sitting through a meeting when I wasn't the one with the problem. I thought, *My dad is the one with the problem!* I've since learned that I was a victim in my mind, and I didn't know how to get my needs met.

My mom came into a small inheritance, and my parents were able to purchase a house in the same neighbourhood where I attended junior high. I attended high school with some of my friends that encompassed several groups from different social classes. One day, two of my friends informed me that I needed to choose them over another group. I told them that was not an option for me, and if they didn't want to be friends with me anymore, that was up to them. To my surprise and delight, they didn't make me choose, and I remained friends with the girls from both groups. This was another defining moment when I was proud that I found the courage to use my voice and stand up for myself.

Mom was a kind, compassionate person and an excellent mother and parent. She took her role very seriously and did the best she knew how. However, she had her own challenges as a child, being diagnosed with *Sydenham's chorea* before she started school and told me she had to be hospitalized for some time and didn't understand why. This disease is an auto-immune disorder also known as St Vitus' Dance and is characterized by rapid, uncoordinated jerking movements primarily affecting the face, hands, and feet. It can result from something as simple as a childhood infection, such as a sore throat and is most common in females from ages five to fifteen. I can only imagine how this must have affected my mom in school and while being around her family and in social settings. I'm certain she noticed how she was different from other people, which created confusion, self-loathing, and a lack of control over her environment.

Over the years, I became truly grateful that I had one parental figure who did not have an addiction and was present. I formed a bond and attachment with my mom, and she served as a strong foundation of support for my siblings and me. We all benefitted from an established routine in other areas of our daily life and knew we could rely on our mom to believe we were safe, loved, and protected despite the absence of our father.

Reflecting back, it doesn't seem like I had much fun growing up, but I did enjoy the times I spent volunteering with my mom. We also did other things together, and mom always did her best to create special days that were fun and exciting. For example, my sister and I were born in December, on the 14th and 18th, and mom moved heaven and earth to throw the best birthday party she could for each of us. She celebrated by making us a cake or cupcakes, and even though we didn't always have friends over, she always hung up a Happy Birthday sign and balloons. We got at least one gift every year, which I know was challenging since our birthdays were so close to Christmas.

As for Christmas, she again did her best to have a tree for us to decorate, and she insisted we wait until after my sister had her birthday, so it didn't take away from her special day. We went to the Army & Navy to purchase tinsel and the LifeSavers Hard Candy Sweet Story Book. My brother and sisters and I had a grand time putting the decorations on the tree, and we added popcorn that we had strung ourselves, along with multicoloured lifesavers and ornaments that we had made at school. We always got a gift, and mom cooked a turkey dinner with all the trimmings year after year.

We didn't take family vacations very often, but when I was around 11 or 12, I recall driving out to Alberta Beach to stay at my aunt's cabin for a few weekends here and there. I loved going to the beach and playing with my cousins. Other times, I visited my grandma's farm for a week or two, and several times my sister joined me. When my grandfather came from Scotland to farm the land, he had to move the rocks, stones, and boulders by hand and with a horse and cart to prepare the soil for planting. We loved the adventure and freedom of being children, using our imaginations to play on the huge rock piles. Sometimes we pretended they were collapsed castles, just waiting for us to bring them to life.

There was one family trip I will never forget that my dad decided to visit his family in eastern Canada. I'm sure he wanted to go alone, but I'm guessing my mom put her foot down, announcing that if he was going east, so was the rest of the family. Mom was allowed one suitcase for her four kids, as well as a cooler and old camp stove to cook on. We packed up my dad's old Plymouth sedan and the seven of us, including an uncle who helped with the driving, travelled over a five-day period to get to our first stop in Kingston, Ontario. I was around twelve, and my sister and brother were eight and five;

Chapter 2

my youngest sister was about three. This was no luxury trip. There was no motel—heck no, not even a tent. We drove night and day and only stopped for gas, pee breaks, and picnic mealtimes along the side of the road. I don't even remember what we ate, but I'm sure it was bologna and cheese sandwiches, crackers, and cheese, and possibly a few pieces of fruit. Occasionally we stopped for a hot meal, and my dad set up the camp stove in the ditch so mom could whip up some wieners and beans or kraft dinner for supper.

I don't know how my mom fed her children three meals a day. There were few fast-food drive-in restaurants and no stores carrying convenience foods like we have today. Quite frankly, I'm not sure how my mother didn't lose her mind. I know there were no seat belts in those days, and we slept in the back seat. My youngest sister was on the floor of the car on one side of the hump, and my brother was on the other side. My other sister and I shared the bench seat with our heads at opposite ends and our feet in each other's faces. We must have stunk to high heaven when we arrived at my aunt's place in Kingston since none of us, including the adults, had the opportunity to bathe for five days.

We stayed with her for a few days, and what I remember the most was being given the task of taking the rest of the kids to the park, along with my male cousin, who was about a year younger. My aunt didn't want all the kids in her house, so a few minutes after we returned from the park, she told us to get out of the house. Kingston is on the eastern end of Lake Ontario at the beginning of the St. Lawrence River, and the park was a few blocks from where they lived. Unfortunately, we couldn't go to the beach because we had too many little ones to look after. My favorite memory of this part of the trip was my cousin and me sleeping in the backyard by ourselves in a tent that my uncle set up.

We moved on to Montreal for the next part of our trip, and I remember being super excited because Expo 67 had taken place the year before, and I anticipated the possibility of seeing *Man and His World*. In my child-like mind, I wished that we could do something for the kids in my family just once. But of course, we did not do anything that took my dad away from spending time drinking with his siblings as it was the one thing that bound them as a family. I remember staying at my uncle's townhouse and meeting a few more aunts, uncles, and cousins. We had some meals and a few good laughs together. I was very upset that we drove all the way to Montreal and didn't even get to drive past *Man and His World*. What I didn't know until years later was that my mom yearned to visit her firstborn son's gravestone in Ontario, and that didn't happen either.

I loved meeting my aunts, uncles, and cousins, and once again, my mom did her best to make our time away as much fun as she could. We played I Spy and other car games and sang a lot of songs during the car ride there and back. And when I returned to school in the fall, I was so excited that I wasn't the only kid in the class who did nothing and went nowhere all summer. I was so proud that I could say I had been on a road trip with my family to Kingston, Ontario and Montreal, Quebec.

Chapter 2

My Recipe For Childhood Blessings

- *Relationships are life's richest gifts; don't take them for granted;*
- *When something doesn't seem right, take action;*
- *Treasure experiences because not all of them are negative;*
- *Experiences help me to be who I am;*
- *Look for the good; it is always there;*
- *Reflect on my actions when I feel important, recognized, and valued.*

My Self-Reflection

Looking back over the years when I was growing up, I'm grateful for all my encounters, good and bad, because they helped me not take people for granted. I learned to recognize that what I was doing helped me view myself as important and valued. I know that the incidents and people who supported me, helped me find the good in life and navigate the dysfunctional pieces. I believe the good outweighed the bad, and because I met incredible people, I had the opportunity to learn valuable lessons along the way. This is why I am the person I am today. I discovered that, like any recipe, I could add an ingredient or two here and there to personalize it.

What is Your Recipe For Childhood Blessings?

Chapter 2

Given Your Recipe, Share Your Self-Reflection

III

Clearing the Weeds of My Mind

> *A soul mate is the one person whose love is powerful enough to motivate you to meet your soul, to do the emotional work of self-discovery, of awakening.*
>
> ~ *Kenny Loggins*

When I was 16, I became immediate friends with a girl I met in my grade ten psychology class at Strathcona High School. I was very naive and hadn't started dating yet; going out consisted of volunteering, going to a friend's house, or babysitting. Having taken care of my siblings, I was in high demand, and I often had to turn parents down. So, when this new friend invited me on a double date, I was both excited and scared to death. Mom surprised me when she said I could go, so I took the bus to my friend's apartment, where she lived with her mom, dad, and sister. I didn't know that my friend was a wild child and dating someone much older. My description of my first date is *a drink with a firehose.*

My friend was surprised to see that I was not wearing makeup, and I had no idea how to put it on. From there, several initiation-like events occurred. The first was having someone else apply makeup on my face. Her boyfriend was from out of town, and he and his friend picked us up in his 1969 Ford Mustang. So, my second initiation was riding in someone else's car because I had only ridden in my dad's or my grandmother's car. I didn't realize I was locking myself into a course of action that could have had serious consequences. However, my adventurous and spontaneous spirit was alive and well, and I didn't think to ask any questions about the plans for the evening. Then, my third initiation occurred when we stopped at the mall located near my house.

    I should have bailed right then and there, but the thrill of the adventure, the fear of missing out, and the need for approval prevented me from backing away. My friend and I sat huddled on a bench while her boyfriend and his friend purchased drugs; I was too naïve to know what kind. This segued into the fourth initiation, which was us piling back into his car and driving to a field at the outskirts of town where several other vehicles stood. The two fellas we were with got out of the car and proceeded to shoot up along with several others.

    Fortunately, no one made my friend or me take any drugs, and no cops showed up. However, I was freaking out on the inside and kicking my ass for not bailing when I had the chance back at the mall. There were times when I was sure I had a guardian angel, and this was one of them. When I thought I had enough initiations for one night, the fellas decided we should go to a dance. It was at a place called the Hub on the university campus. I recall that there was no age restriction because they weren't allowed to serve alcohol. Someone passed me a paper cup, and I took a big gulp. It was coke spiked with rum, and it burned down my throat. Obviously, not serving alcohol didn't prevent people from sneaking in their own. The best part of my *first date* was the band, the dancing, and the rock and roll music. I loved it! I was having so much fun and didn't want to leave. However, my intuition told me I was in over my head and getting drunk was not a wise choice.

I was relieved that we dropped off her boyfriend's friend on the way back to her apartment. When we got to her place, I found myself in another uncomfortable position. It seemed like an exposure rather than an initiation. My friend and her boyfriend were making out in the front seat. I sat in the back, not knowing whether to stand outside in the middle of the night or just sit through it. I'm sure they didn't make out all the way, but this was the first time I had witnessed a couple in lust for each other. I chose to sit through it the same way I always managed uncomfortable situations. I remember thinking, *You've been here in many other different situations before; block it out, put up the wall, this is no time for emotions, and you'll get through it. You always do.* In my wildest dreams, I never expected to be initiated into sex, drugs, and rock n' roll all in one night.

We were friends for many years, and I also became a wild child for a short while. I got myself into all kinds of ridiculous and dangerous situations. I craved adventure and became a thrill-seeker, taking way too many risks while seeking the approval of others. Some included hitchhiking all over the city of Edmonton, making fake ID's, so I could get into clubs, riding in a stolen car, sneaking out of my bedroom window at night to meet up with friends, stealing merchandise from a few stores, drinking, and experimenting with drugs. Fortunately for me, I never liked how I behaved under the influence of drugs and how it hampered my ability to think for myself. I now realize that children who grow up in an alcoholic home become impulsive. And just like on my drinking-from-a-firehose first date, I tended to throw caution to the wind, locking myself into a course of action without considering the consequences. As a result, there were many times I was confused and extremely critical for not controlling my environment. I also spent an excessive amount of energy cleaning up my messes.

On July 24, 1974, my wild child friend invited me to the annual ten-day Klondike Days exhibition held in Edmonton. Initially, I said no because I had taken in the fair's sights, sounds, and smells several times, but then, my spontaneous, adventurous side won. A group of eleven of us met at the fairgrounds, and I remember meeting this tall, blue-eyed guy with sandy hair. Be still my beating heart—there was an immediate connection, and my heart went pitter-pat. I was twitter-pated! We all decided to go to the beer gardens, and I ended up sitting at the opposite end of the table from him. Since we were a large group and didn't all want to do the same activities, we decided to split up.

I figured I'd never see him again, but near closing time several hours later as I walked down the midway, who should appear but the guy who made my heart go pitter-pat. I ran and jumped up, throwing my legs and arms around him without any hesitation. I planted a kiss on his cheek and whispered in his ear, *I thought I was never going to see you again.* It was one of the most spontaneous moves I had ever made—not stopping to think and acting only on my intuition at that moment. In the movie Jerry Maguire, Dorothy Boyd says to Jerry, *Shut up, just shut up. You had me at hello.* If my husband were to share his side of this story, he might say, *You had me at the jump.*

In the summer of 1975, the guy who made my heart go pitter-pat joined the army and took basic training in Cornwallis, Nova Scotia. We continued a long-distance relationship by phone and then decided to do something crazy and romantic by getting engaged in Montreal, Quebec on October 10, 1975. After completing his basic training, he was posted to Calgary,

Chapter 3

Alberta, and on April 10, 1976, we had a small ceremony and were married on the base. We started our life together in a tiny, dingy basement suite in Calgary, but several months later, we were able to move into the PMQs—Private Married Quarters. I didn't know it at the time, but my husband was to become one of my greatest teachers.

As a newly married couple, I believe a simple poster my sister gave us as a wedding present perfectly describes our jumping-off point. It came with us to every single home we move to, including a holiday trailer; we always found a wall to hang it on. The poster was entitled, *Rules for a Happy Marriage*, and it became the foundation we turned to as a young couple learning to create a partnership. We treated the rules like a recipe, memorized them, and focused our attention on living our lives in line with them.

1. Never both be angry at the same time;
2. Never yell at each other unless the house is on fire;
3. If one of you has to win an argument, let it be your mate;
4. If you have to criticize, do it lovingly;
5. Never bring up mistakes of the past;
6. Neglect the whole world rather than each other;
7. Never go to sleep with an argument unsettled;
8. At least once every day, try to say one kind or complimentary thing to your life's partner;
9. When you have done something wrong, be ready to admit it and ask for forgiveness;
10. It takes two to make a quarrel, and the one in the wrong is the one who does the most talking.

Evolving To Be Me

A little over a year after we were married, a defining moment changed my behaviour forever. The army and the base put on a family day every few years, and several of my husband's family members came to visit that year. All the men went to the base to learn about the military equipment, and the gals, which consisted of my mother-in-law, sister-in-law, and me, stayed behind to prepare dinner and engage in girl talk. Shortly after the men left the house, I got a phone call from one of my best friends. She asked me to drive her and her boyfriend to the airport because her future father-in-law was in critical condition in a hospital in Timmons, Ontario, and they were flying out to pay their last respects.

Since I was constantly seeking approval from others, especially my in-laws, I told a lie when I could have easily told the truth. My sister and mother-in-law wanted to come along for the ride, and my friend and her boyfriend were not married. I knew my mother-in-law disapproved of unmarried couples travelling together, and I wanted her blessing. So, I told my mother-in-law something I thought she wanted to hear regarding why we were taking them to the airport. I don't recall exactly what I said, but it was a lie, and at the time, I thought it was no big deal.

I was shocked that evening when our family sat in our living room, and my father-in-law asked his wife what we did for the day. My mother-in-law replied by telling him that we drove one of my friends to the airport and proceeded to explain why—the reason I had given her—the lie. Her answer didn't make sense to my husband, so he questioned me in front of his entire family. I didn't know what to say but knew I was caught in a lie, so I gave him the look, and he got the message and changed the subject. Later, I shared the real reason why I drove my friend to the airport because I didn't want to start our life together with a lie.

Chapter 3

This is an example of a time when I wished there was a lever I could have pulled, dropping the floor out from under me and taking me with it. I was so embarrassed that I wanted to disappear. I was sick inside, wanting to throw up from the disgust and betrayal I caused myself, my husband, and his family. I was deeply ashamed and knew I wanted to be proud, so I committed never to lie again. I vowed to live my life with integrity, which meant keeping my word and following through on my promises. It also included treating myself and others with kindness and respect and showing up and behaving in a way that nurtures and supports my relationships, work, and self-esteem. When I made this pledge to myself, life became so much easier because I didn't have to remember what I said yesterday and could move forward with a clear conscience.

This incident made me recognize that, before it happened, I didn't know what normal behaviour was, and my family was not always honest. I learned to lie and keep secrets out of fear of what others thought. I didn't know my truth or who I was, and there were times when I lied because I was embarrassed. The repercussion was that I then judged myself without mercy.

My husband and I had a lot of fun during the first five years we were married, partying quite a bit and travelling to Edmonton often to visit family. In many ways, we grew up together, and we sometimes spent money foolishly. I learned how to be an army wife because my husband was away on exercise about 80 percent of the time. In 1978, he was on a six-month UN tour in Cypress, and the wives were allowed to fly via the Canadian armed forces to meet their husbands in Lahr, Germany for two weeks. It was the trip of a lifetime, riding in a Hercules helicopter and visiting several different countries in Europe. This was the honeymoon we never had.

Another defining moment was when my husband and I

joined a network marketing company that same year. We read hundreds of books, attended conventions, and purchased many different recorded series by inspirational speakers. At one of the conventions, a speaker said something I have not forgotten: *Your life will change by the books you read, the people you associate with, and what you feed your mind.* He referred to what you watch and listen to—garbage in, garbage out! He inspired me to consciously choose the books I read, the people I associated with, and what I watched and listened to. I desired to become a happier, more educated, and positive person, so I chose to spend my lunch and coffee breaks reading in a quiet place away from others. A few of the books I read were: *The Road Less Traveled, Think and Grow Rich, You Can't Steal Second with Your Foot on First, The Power of Positive Thinking,* and *The Magic of Thinking Big.* Personal growth became something I valued and have remained passionate about from that day forward.

A motivational speaker, Skip Ross, created a talk entitled *Dynamic Living,* and in the early 80s, we purchased his series of tapes. It was a formula for living that I listened to hundreds of times. Skip also wrote a book entitled, *Say Yes to Your Potential,* and one of the concepts that resonated with me was, *The environment and experiences I grew up in have not made me the way I am, but they did form powerful patterns of thought in my subconscious mind, and habitual ways of thinking about myself. Although these experiences influence who we think we are, we are not locked into any image of the past. We have been made to believe we are the way we are because of past programming, but we can change our patterns, behaviours, and beliefs.*[4]

The author also tells a story about how our mind is like a garden, and if our mind is filled with negative thoughts, our

---

[4] https://skipross.com/

Chapter 3

outcome in life is not going to be positive. I was aware I had a victim mentality, and my self-talk was negative. The Dynamic Living Formula included ten principles for living. One of the principles was, *Give, and you will receive*.[5] An action step I realized I could implement was always give a word of praise, although it took me some time to gain the courage to provide others with this gift. It was initially awkward because I cared too much about what people thought. However, I eventually found my voice and looked for ways to implement this principle. Adopting the concept that I was not locked into the past and could choose to give the word of praise gave me the confidence to continue planting positive thoughts and become a happier person. The books I read, the people I met, and the conferences I attended helped me change my thinking and patterned behaviour. I have been on a path of spiritual growth ever since.

One of the first speakers my husband and I went to see was a very young Bob Proctor, who gave us two takeaways from this event, *Change is inevitable but personal growth is a choice*,[6] along with several cassette tapes we purchased with relaxation instructions that we listened to in bed every night. Acting on these incentives inspired us to change our life together, establish good sleep practices and make personal growth a priority.

I've heard that things can get worse before they get better, and that seemed to be our reality from 1980 to 1990. I believe my husband and I were tilling the soil, planting healthy seeds, falling down, and getting up. We won, and sometimes, we lost, but we grew both individually and together. I had accumulated a lot of negativities over my first twenty years, and my mind

---

[5] Ibid

[6] https://www.proctorgallagherinstitute.com/

was like a garden filled with weeds. Through the self-work I did, I became aware of this and understood that I was the only one who could change my thoughts, stories, and beliefs.

My enabling patterns continued in my marriage within situations where I assumed I needed to organize my behaviour around the needs and choices of my husband. Although my husband wasn't an alcoholic, I always seemed to step in to fix or solve problems or make their consequences disappear. For example, finances were always a problem. It seemed I was always trying to mend our poor spending habits by working harder, depriving myself of buying anything and taking on the responsibility of our financial situation as my problem to solve.

Although joining a network marketing company positively affected our lives, it also had drawbacks due to our poor relationship with money and my codependent behaviour. We did not have a handle on our finances and always spent more than we made. We charged our credit cards to purchase books, tapes, and products, and pay for travel expenses related to conventions and conferences. We bought into the *fake it until you make it* mindset, and in 1980 I supported my husband in his decision not to renew his contract with the military. Our goal was to earn a living through network marketing, even though we didn't have an extensive network or a steady income.

We didn't have a plan or a budget, and we lived like gypsies, flying by the seat of our pants. Once he left the military, we no longer had his stable income to fall back on, and we could no longer live in a PMQ. For the first time in five years, we found ourselves moving several times, searching for an ideal rental property. We moved into our second rental when I was six months pregnant with our daughter, and two months later, our landlord decided he wanted to live in the house and asked us to move out. My husband had taken on a job driving for a

Chapter 3

courier company, and his dad asked if he wanted to join him in his construction business in Edmonton. I was nine months pregnant at this time, and we simultaneously decided to attend a network marketing convention in Edmonton during the Thanksgiving weekend our daughter was due. We figured babies are never born on their due date, and since we were moving there, we may as well look for a house to rent. We were convinced we could build a network marketing business once we relocated. Maybe most babies are not born on their due date, but our precious daughter was born on Saturday, October 10, 1981, at eight o'clock in the morning. When my husband called his parents from the hospital to tell them they had a granddaughter, they thought we were still asleep in their basement. Several hours after I delivered our daughter, the nurses permitted me to attend the evening festivities of the convention, making me promise not to have a drop of alcohol.

We returned to Calgary nine days after our daughter was born, packed up our belongings, rented a truck that my husband and I drove to Edmonton, and had my brother drive our car. It was overwhelming to think that we were moving all our worldly possessions, including a dog and cat, and renting a house without a steady income. However, due to our dire situation, a new landlord gave us the benefit of the doubt and rented us a two-bedroom house on the spot in a new subdivision that we could move into that night.

My husband worked in his dad's construction business for several months when the recession hit, and his dad lost all his contracts in one day. We found ourselves in a real pickle as we couldn't afford to pay our rent or buy groceries. We ended up moving into my parents' basement suite. Here I was 29 years old, with a new baby, without a pot to pee in or a window to throw in out of. I was so ashamed but didn't know how to articulate my feelings or express my emotions to anyone. However, I was grateful for the support from both of our families.

Several months later, my husband's parents were hired as groundskeepers and maintenance staff near a provincial park several miles from Rocky Mountain House in Alberta. This gave us the opportunity to move into their house and support my brother-in-law. He was about 12 at the time and could continue his education at a Christian school while staying with us. We kept an eye on their place, and although I was more than grateful to them, caring for a pre-teen and a new baby was sometimes astounding. On top of that, my husband's parents always had an open-door policy, with family members dropping in unannounced. There was also the additional stress of not being able to move our possessions into various rooms in the house because my mother and father-in-law had not officially moved out.

My husband got his class-one license and was on the road driving truck. All day-to-day decisions fell on my shoulders, but what I didn't realize was that I was still responding from a state of dysfunction, making choices around the needs of my husband and others. Several months later, my mother and father-in-law decided to sell their home, and the realtor told them their house could sell faster if it were empty. From the first uncalculated risk during the summer of 1980 when I supported my husband to decide not to renew his contract with the military, we moved too many times to count. We continued making poor decisions during those years, like having a baby without a steady income or stable living arrangements. Through to 1983, we continued to struggle financially and take more risks without any game plan, which left me immersed in more shame and blaming my husband and others for our situation.

During this period in our marriage, I was humiliated and

remorseful about our circumstances. I had no idea why life was such a struggle, nor did I understand how I was recreating some of the same patterns I witnessed and adopted growing up. I carried the coping behaviours I picked up in childhood into adulthood.

About a year later, I was expecting our son, and my husband's parents, who were still groundskeepers, informed him they were hiring salespeople to sell memberships. Although I said nothing, I truly resented his parents at this time because I had to find someone to look after our daughter, given I was working full-time and had to figure out how to cope with my husband working out of town. When it was time for me to go on maternity leave for my son, my mother and father-in-law suggested I come and help in the country store on weekends. I could work in exchange for the help they gave us, and my two sisters-in-law helped me pack up our belongings and put them in storage. Once again, I believed it was my responsibility to do the heavy lifting and hard work. My mother and father-in-law loaned us the money to purchase a used holiday trailer that we parked on the property they were maintaining, and we lived in it, agreeing to make monthly payments. I did help in the country store and delivered our son several months later at the Rocky Mountain House Hospital.

My mother-in-law was graceful, helpful, and very supportive. In fact, I'm sure she kept me from going squirrelly. It was a stressful time being so dependent on my husband's parents and not having any outside interests, projects, or friends. Then, my father-in-law's employment situation changed, and they began looking to purchase a house in the area. My husband and I knew the writing was on the wall, and it was time to stand on our own two feet. He re-applied to the Canadian Armed Forces when our son was about nine months old. His re-engagement was accepted around the same time my mother and father-in-law moved into their new home. One of the purchasing conditions was to include the holiday trailer we had lived in as part of their down payment. When I look back on this time, I see that our poor financial decisions combined with the uncalculated risks we took put us in this situation. We needed to take responsibility, be grateful for the help we received along the way and forgive ourselves and our loved ones. We don't always see things the same way, and sometimes it's best to turn the page on the past and move on.

The re-engagement process happened rather fast, and it seemed that one minute we were living close to our in-laws with our babies in Rocky Mountain House in a holiday trailer, and the next minute we were moving into a PMQ. My head was spinning because it seemed to happen so fast. The next thing I knew, my husband was being deployed to Cyprus for a six-month peace-keeping mission. We decided to claim bankruptcy just before he left for Cyprus. I was expected to file monthly reports to our trustee, and it didn't make sense financially for me to work because our son was ten months, and our daughter was two-and-a-half years old. Once again, I was expected to clean up the mess, and I sensed the weight of the whole world on my shoulders.

While my husband was away, my young children and I spent weekends and holidays at my in-laws' acreage. Because they still maintained an open-door policy for family members, one never knew who might be visiting at any given time. On one occasion, several family members rented some trikes; they were motorized, three-wheel, all-terrain vehicles that are now illegal to operate due to all the fatal accidents they caused. After some time riding around on bush trails, they suggested that one of my sister-in-law's and I give it a try. I was very nervous

Chapter 3

but witnessed my younger sister-in-law taking a leisurely ride around the garden patch and thought, *How hard can it be.* My children were taking a nap, so I knew I had some free time, and I was yearning to do something spontaneous. My inner voice shouted, *Where is your sense of adventure?* I was excited and threw caution to the wind, jumping on that trike and headed off down the road. I didn't think to wear a helmet or protective clothing, and I had no idea where the gas and brakes were. I certainly underestimated my reflexes when it came to riding a vehicle I had never ridden before.

It turns out I mistook the brake for the gas and didn't know how to stop. As a result, I drove right into a tree. The good news was that I didn't hit my head or face, but the bad news was that the steel peg I had my foot on dug into my calf and left me with a serious deep gash in my right leg. I was fortunate that my older sister-in-law was a nurse and arrived on the scene within seconds. She loaded me into the back of a pick-up truck on a makeshift stretcher, and off to the hospital we went, lickety-split! She remained by my side during the ride and while they stitched up my severed muscle and my leg. I recall not having much freezing or sedation and squeezing her hand as if my life depended on it. Unfortunately, my little sense of adventure put me in the hospital for eight days and left my mother and father-in-law looking after our children.

This took place in the 80s, so there was no text messaging, email, or cell phones, so when my husband called our number on the good old landline, there was no answer, and he was worried. He called his parents to find out where I was, and his commanding officer concluded I had family support because my in-laws were looking after our children while I was in the hospital. In my world, I wished the military could have sent my husband home because I was still recovering and didn't have that same support when I returned to Calgary. Years ago, there was an advertisement for the military using the phrase, *There is no life like it*. Well, that's for sure! I've often heard military wives quip half-jokingly that if the military wanted you to have a wife and kids, they would have issued them. Once back in Calgary with my kids, I did manage with the help of my sister and brother-in-law, and my mom sent my brother to stay with me because I couldn't drive for several weeks. My husband didn't arrive home for another three months.

I encountered life like a ping-pong ball the first few years of my children's lives, reacting negatively, behaving like a victim, and believing life had to be a difficult struggle. Within all these scenarios, what I find curious is that I continued to act the way I had growing up, not speaking up for myself because I was too afraid to create conflict. It seemed easier to adapt my behaviour to what I thought others expected. But did they? I began asking myself questions like, *When will you let go of your frustration, assuming you are not appreciated and that you don't matter? What pieces of myself am I losing when I behave this way?*

Chapter 3

My Recipe For Clearing the Weeds of My Mind

- *Commit to Rules for a Happy Marriage[7];*
- *Accept that things may get worse before they get better;*
- *Believe my life can improve;*
- *Take responsibility for my role in every situation;*
- *Believe in others;*
- *Be willing to work on me and not try to fix my husband;*
- *Accept support from family and friends.*

My Self-Reflection

The first few years of our marriage were no picnic, and it seemed like a journey through the dark night of my soul. I didn't know how messed up our life was or why. I realize now that it is normal for adult children of alcoholics to lock themselves into a course of action without considering alternative behaviours or possible consequences. There were many times when I believed I was completely out of control. However, despite our poor decisions and lack of awareness, we continued to move forward. We learned from our mistakes, remembered the Rules of a Happy Marriage, planted a few new seeds along the way, and became grateful for the support from others.

---

[5] Ibid

Evolving To Be Me

What is Your Recipe For Clearing the Weeds of Your Mind?

Chapter 3

Given Your Recipe, Share Your Self-Reflection

IV

So What!—Now What?

*Progress is rarely a straight line. There are
Always bumps in the road, but you can
make the choice to keep looking ahead.*

~ Kara Goucher

My husband participated in many of the customs practised in the Canadian Armed Forces. In the 1980s, most of them involved celebrating one thing or another and drinking to excess. One of the events took place after my husband returned from Cyprus when our daughter was about three years old. My husband and his buddy consumed 40 ounces of hard liquor and proceeded to drive the car while impaired. My mom was visiting for the weekend, and when my husband showed up recklessly drunk shortly after she arrived, I was embarrassed and angry. However, I didn't have to say anything because he got his wake-up call when our daughter looked out the window and, in her innocent toddler voice, said, *Daddy, you don't park a car like that!* He had parked the car sideways in the driveway. It was a defining moment in both our lives as he never got that recklessly drunk again.

Life ticked along with no dramatic events or financial strife until one summer in 1985 when we attended our family's annual camp-out in Buffalo Lake. When we left Calgary after work on Friday night, our station wagon was packed to the ceiling with our toddlers, dog, cat, and camping gear. The camp-out took place in an area where my husband had grown up and spent a lot of summers with his siblings, aunts, uncles, and cousins. The location changed that year, so my husband needed directions. As we got closer to the lake, it seemed like we were going in circles and not getting close to our destination. My husband was so upset that he wanted to rip the steering wheel out. Riding in the car for several hours with him in that state was hell, and nothing I could say calmed him down.

My husband was an excellent infanteer and highly trained in orienteering—navigating with a map and compass. Being lost in this part of Alberta created a lot of stress for him, and it kicked the legs out from under his pride; he didn't handle it well. Until later, neither of us knew that the directions he was given were only correct if you were coming from Edmonton. Once my husband realized this, we arrived at our destination ten minutes later. I find that life is funny that way; once I know what direction I'm coming from, I can arrive at my destination much quicker and with less tension.

Since we arrived in the dark, we stayed in the car for the night because it was too late to set up the tent. Neither one of us slept well, especially my husband, given he was up walking around with chest pains most of the night. I got my children up and dressed for breakfast in the morning, but my husband was in too much pain to eat. We decided to pack up and head back to Calgary. At a junction on Highway 21, I asked him what he wanted to do? We could either go right to go home

Chapter 4

or left to the hospital in Stettler. We decided to go left to the hospital because his arms were so numb, he could barely hold the steering wheel.

Our family was overwhelmed as we waited for a doctor to come and tell us the results of his blood tests. He couldn't get my husband admitted fast enough because he concluded that he had a heart attack. An indication of a heart attack is enzymes in the blood from the damaged heart muscle. I wondered how this was possible, given he was only thirty years old. Not knowing what to do, I phoned my mother-in-law in Edmonton, and she suggested I call her sister, who lived in Stettler, to ask if my children and I could stay with her.

I am eternally grateful to my husband's aunt, who took us in with no questions asked, allowing us to stay with her until the doctors made some decisions. When my sister-in-law, who is a nurse, heard what happened, she phoned her brother in the hospital. She suggested that he have a conversation with his doctor about the importance of being transferred to a hospital in Calgary where he lived and could receive the best medical care, education, and training. This one significant decision would help ensure he never had another heart attack. If the doctor disagreed with the hospital transfer, she was prepared to come to Stettler with the necessary equipment, oxygen tanks, and defibrillator to pick him up at the hospital and drive him to Calgary in the back of our station wagon.

Had this incident occurred while my husband was on duty, he would have been required to see an army medic. I realized I needed to be vulnerable and do my part to ensure he got the best medical care possible. I mustered up the courage to telephone someone in authority in the military and requested that my husband be transferred to the hospital in Calgary. There wasn't a resounding *yes* from the military officer, and it was a wait-and-see situation. All our family members were on pins and needles, wanting to hear the verdict.

My mom heard about our situation and wanted to help by coming for my children because she thought this might give me more freedom to visit my husband and take care of necessary errands. I told her I didn't think it was a good idea to take the kids away from me when their dad was in the hospital. However, it didn't seem to matter what I said to my mother because she and my sister arrived in Stettler several hours later to pick up my kids. I was overwhelmed and frustrated because I had no say in the matter. As I stood in the doorway, watching them drive away, I was aware of how lost and scared I was.

Within a few minutes, one of my husband's aunts, who worked at the hospital, arrived to let us know they were moving my husband to Calgary by ambulance. Of course, I thanked both my husband's aunts profusely, packed up my belongings, and drove our station wagon with the dog back home. On top of all this confusion, we also lost our cat. It was hard to believe that our family had left for a simple family weekend camping trip only two days earlier.

My children had been in my mom's care for about a week when several traumatic events took place. Mom did not drive and relied on her children to do so. She could not care for her grandchildren during the day because she had her own business cleaning homes. My youngest sister, who was 21, worked at a daycare and took her niece and nephew to work. She informed me that my son was shut in a closet and could not get out for many hours. When he was finally found, they could tell he had been sobbing his little heart out and eventually fell asleep.

The day arrived when my mom and siblings brought our children back home, and I was overjoyed with the anticipation of their arrival. Several hours after they were supposed to arrive,

Chapter 4

one of my sisters-in-law called to check in. When I told her they weren't there yet, she indicated that if it was her, she might check herself into a mental health facility. At the time, I was fretting and worried to bits, wondering why they were taking so long. Little did I know that my brother, sisters, mom, and children had been in a car accident while driving through a rainstorm on their way to Calgary from Edmonton. I can only imagine the trauma my children went through. There was no seat belt law at the time, and the RCMP officer told my brother it was an absolute miracle no one was injured. I was grateful to everyone in the car that day for their ceaseless praying and that no one was hurt, thanks to my brother, who has exceptional defensive driving skills.

My kids and I were out for a walk in our neighbourhood several weeks after they arrived home, and we walked by a huge pile of grass clippings. Both of my children started crying, running, and screaming, *The dump hill, the dump hill.* I was frantic and shocked, wondering what had taken place to cause my children to have this traumatic reaction to a pile of grass clippings. They were too young and emotionally distraught to explain what was wrong, so I immediately contacted my sister to learn that a staff member at the daycare had taken several children to the cemetery across the street for a walk. According to my sister, the staff person pointed out a recently dug grave that included a pile of grass clippings and told my children that their father could be buried in a grave like this one. I have to remind myself that this was the 80s, and the daycare staff there did not have to have any formal training. However, I know in my heart of hearts that my mom, sisters, and brother were trying to help the best way they knew how.

Several months after my husband's heart attack, we decided to purchase a half-duplex with the financial assistance of a sister and brother-in-law. Our finances were somewhat stable, so we laid down some roots and planned some fun family activities with family and friends. We began acting like grownups and lived there for several years until my husband was posted to Regina, Saskatchewan. A Canadian Armed Forces member assigned from one position to another is entitled to relocation benefits, including covering the costs of relocating the family to their new location. This is often referred to as a house-hunting trip. Before we left on our house-hunting trip, we chose to sell our half-duplex and look for a house to purchase in Regina. Prior to leaving, I prepared resumes to drop off to potential employers, so we could qualify for a mortgage. The events that took place next were proof that the new seeds I had planted in the garden of my mind—the thoughts, behaviours, and beliefs—were working. We looked at houses, put in an offer, and I went on interviews, got a job, and found a babysitter in five short days. One of the affirmations I heard from *The Dynamic Living tape series was Faith is the substance of things hoped for, the evidence of things not seen.*[8] I wrote out pages and pages of this scripture the night before my last interview. The next day we found out I got the job and could take possession of the house we put the offer on.

We moved into the four-level split home, settled into family life, and had lots of fun adventures with our neighbours, friends, and visiting family. One of my husband's cousins and her husband lived in the same city, and he was a pastor. We were blessed to attend their church, spend time with them, and made friends with many members of the church family. We enrolled our children in various activities like T-ball, swimming, and piano lessons, and even built a rink in the

---

[8] The Bible, Hebrews 11:1, NKJV

Chapter 4

backyard to see what they might be interested in. As a result, we learned our daughter was creative and independent, and our son loved skateboarding.

I recognized I was starting to find my voice, stand up for myself, and take responsibility for the roles I played in most situations. Since my husband's position had unique hours, and he worked some evenings and all weekends, I was left to parent our children and make daily decisions. One typical Saturday, my kids and I were figuring out what we wanted to do for the day. My son and I did not have the best relationship, and we had an argument. He was screaming at the top of his lungs, *I hate you, I hate you, I hate you,* while he stood pounding his fists on the other side of the basement door. I was heartbroken because it was the last thing I wanted to hear because at the same time he spewed those words out at me, I was thinking the same about him. Waves of shame washed over me as I concluded I was a terrible mother.

This question flashed through my mind, *If you don't do something to have a better relationship with your son now, what will your relationship look like in ten years?* The family resource centre offered a course entitled *Self Esteem and the Family*, and I enrolled immediately. It was my first step toward understanding that I had adopted parenting styles from my parents, such as yelling, not always listening, and not giving my children words of praise.

I implemented these new tools by praising them, encouraging them to talk about their feelings, and letting them know how proud I was of them. Each night at bedtime, I read them a story and said, *If I had to line up all the little boys and girls in the world and only pick one son or daughter, I would pick you because you are very special to me.* I knew these new practices were working because when my parents came for a visit, my mom asked what had happened to her grandson. I told her it was his mother who needed some training in order to create a better relationship with her son.

A quote I heard by Jackie Kennedy during my early parenting days became my compass, *If you bungle raising your children, I don't think whatever else you do matters very much.* Many years later, I applied for a promotion at work and didn't get it. Several days later, my 21-year-old son and I were out for lunch, and I said I was extremely upset because, *I just want to be number one at something* to which he replied, *Your number one to me, Mom.* To this day, I still get teary-eyed, thinking about what might have happened if I hadn't used Jackie Kennedy's quote as a compass for raising my children.

Since my husband worked most weekends, my children and I got groceries and ran errands. I dreaded taking them anywhere because they were young and often out of control in a store. I knew I needed to do something about their behaviour and implement logical consequences to fit their actions. One Saturday afternoon, I had my first opportunity when we entered an extremely busy supermarket. Looking both my children, aged five and seven, in the eye, I said, *No acting up in any way in this store, or we will go home without the groceries, and you will have no supper.* I located one of the few available grocery carts and proceeded to the fish counter.

When I turned around to put the fish in the cart, I was shocked that my son had returned it to the front of the store. I calmly returned the fish to the butcher, marched my children out of the store to the car, and drove them home. That evening, we all went to bed with no supper, and some may think this was harsh. However, my children knew I loved them, that I did not tolerate poor behaviour, and I meant what I said. They did not misbehave in a store from that day forward.

Chapter 4

In 1990, my husband wanted to further his education and go back to school to study computer science, so he chose to put in his release from the Military. Several weeks later, after careful consideration, he decided to retract his release. He was informed that his position had been filled, and he was redeployed to Victoria, BC. Although we loved our two years in Regina, and my husband was promoted to sergeant there, we had a few memories we were happy to leave behind. Our daughter was diagnosed with asthma, and to get the medication into her lungs faster, she had to use a nebulizer. It's a machine that changes the medication from a liquid to a mist. She was also hospitalized for several days because she had a severe asthma attack after returning from a camping trip with her friend's family. As parents of a seven-year-old, we were extremely worried about her health. Our children lacked social skills and didn't make friends easily because they had poor self-esteem. We received our daughter's report card at the end of her grade-three year and the teacher informed us that she had a speech impediment and advised us that she needed speech therapy.

We sold our four-level-split in the summer of 1990, and while on another house-hunting trip, we purchased a home that was a handyman's special. We stayed in a motel until we took possession of our house and our furniture arrived. While staying in the motel, my husband left for Gage Town, New Brunswick for an eight-week small-arms instructors course. When I went to enrol my children in school, I showed the principal my daughter's report card, indicating she needed speech therapy. His response was, *Let's take a wait-and-see approach*. We never heard anyone else tell us our daughter needed speech therapy and I will be forever grateful for the principal's response. While in the office, I was asked to become part of the parent education advisory council. Participating in the PEAC and getting involved with my children's education provided the opportunity to meet other parents, learn what was going on at the school and in the district first-hand. While my husband was away on his course, I enrolled in a parenting class at the school called *How to Talk so Kids will Listen & Listen so Kids will Talk,* modelled after the book by the same name by Adele Faber and Elaine Mazlish. It had a profound effect on my relationship with my children.

I applied at a temporary agency, Kelly Girl, because I knew I needed to work, and I had an interview the same day our furniture arrived. Somehow, I managed to get to the interview and was immediately offered a temporary position for a crown corporation called BC Systems. After the assignment was over, Kelly Girl sent me to another interview for a temporary position working as an administrative assistant for the director of Voice Telecommunications.

After working for several weeks for the director, who was a female engineer, the position was posted as a permanent position, and several staff members encouraged me to apply. I was apprehensive because rumour had it that no one wanted to work for her; she was very direct and not at all personable. However, I did apply and got the job. There were many days I knew I was in over my head, knowing nothing about the telecommunications industry. As her administrative assistant, I was required to take minutes at meetings and support seven managers and fifty support staff. About a year after I started working for her, she commented, *You are a square peg in a round hole.*

I had worked as an administrative assistant for lawyers, accountants, and vice presidents of insurance companies and had great relationships with bosses and co-workers and received excellent references. However, I still viewed myself as a victim, had low self-esteem, and judged myself harshly. Although I had been changing my thoughts, stories, and beliefs, I realized I had more personal work to do. I was still trying to conform to my environment, push myself up a rope, or to put it another way, dim my light and hide by stuffing myself into a corner. I became aware I had spent most of my life trying to fit in instead of standing out and being me. I was always afraid of doing something wrong in school, being laughed at and ridiculed by teachers and students. I thought if I conformed to the way others wanted me to be, I could do better and be better. Although her statement hurt, I asked myself if it was true?

In September 1990, when my husband returned from his small arms instructors' course in Gagetown, New Brunswick, he learned that the third battalion of the Princess Patricia's Canadian Light Infantry was designated as the fast response unit for the first gulf war.

Since my husband's heart attack, he had only been given support duties rather than combat roles, so he was not up to speed on the latest operational procedures. He didn't think learning them on a flight to war was fair to the troops he was to lead. He recognized it was a stressful situation all around, and after an interview with the battalion commander, he marked my husband's contract as *Services No Longer Required.*

My husband qualified for retraining through the employment insurance program and enrolled in the Business Machines Technician Course at Camosun College, starting in September 1991. While my husband was home one afternoon in August, a neighbourhood kid knocked on the door to report that our daughter was hit by a car while riding her bike. She had to have pins put in her arm. I was at work and came home to find a note on the door indicating my family was at the hospital. I was in a state of panic and shock. Both my husband and I were overwhelmed and didn't handle the situation in the best possible way. I know we did the best we could as parents, but I realize now that I just wanted to run and hide. As a result, I didn't think about any possible long-term consequences of the accident for our daughter. Neither my husband nor I thought to contact the insurance company to hold the driver of the car accountable. We did not insist that she have routine check-ups to ensure her injuries weren't anything more than a broken arm.

At the time of this writing, our daughter is in her early forties and still has migraines. I often wonder if they are related to this accident that took place many years ago. My daughter and I have talked about her childhood, and I have shared the areas where she faced some trauma growing up. I have apologized for not being there for her in the way she needed me to be. I have since learned that when I know better, I do better.

Two impactful decisions my husband I made had a far-reaching positive effect on our children. We were truly blessed to be able to send them to Alberta for several weeks every summer. They were able to stay with their grandparents in Rocky Mountain House and with my mom and sister in Edmonton. They were also able to visit and get to know some of their aunts, uncles, and cousins. The second decision we made was when our son was ten years old; we recognized he was addicted to the television, and it affected his grades and behaviour. We made what some parents may call a drastic choice and gave away our TV. Our children became very resourceful with how they spent their time, and it gave us the opportunity to be more active as a family. To this day, our son says this was the best decision we could have made at the time for our family.

One of the many parenting books we read was *Kids Are*

Chapter 4

Worth It by Barbara Coloroso. She had six critical messages children need to hear from their parents. These messages were like a recipe I could follow, so I posted them on our refrigerator while my children were growing up.

1. *I believe in you;*
2. *I trust you;*
3. *I know you can handle this;*
4. *You are listened to;*
5. *You are cared for;*
6. *You are very important to me.*[9]

I had been working for the director for a couple of years when I received a call from my doctor's office asking me to make an appointment. While sitting in his office, I was surprised, when he asked me the following questions, *Have you ever used heroin or other types of opioids? Have you had multiple sex partners?* He moved on to ask me medical history questions. I didn't realize that he was trying to make a diagnosis. I only had routine blood work; therefore, I didn't know there was anything to diagnose. Much later, I learned the importance of asking my doctor questions. However, at the time, I was in shock and didn't even know if or what I should ask. He referred me to a gastroenterologist.

It was the gastroenterologist who informed me that I needed to go to the hospital to have a liver biopsy. I was a busy wife and mother and chauffeur and cook for my family. I worked full time and didn't think I had time to spend on an overnight stay at the hospital. In fact, one of my friends who knew me very well made a joke, saying, *Debra's idea of slowing*

---

[9] http://www.kidsareworthit.com/

down is checking in to the hospital for a liver biopsy. I returned to his office a few weeks later to be told I had primary biliary cholangitis and might need a liver transplant by the time I was 60. Some people's initial reaction after receiving a frightening diagnosis is a feeling of being overwhelmed and feeling numb. My response was quite pragmatic, *It's no big deal.* It seemed like light years into the future at the time, so I carried on with my life—business, as usual, so to speak. Most people move into a degree of shock, often not even knowing what they are feeling or thinking. They have no idea what action to take, with several thoughts going through their mind. *Why me?* Some have feelings of overwhelm, being pissed off, or crave isolation and want to crawl under the covers in bed and never come out. Over time, I had all those feelings and learned they were normal. Many times, I slowed down and told myself, *Take a breath, a deep breath. Take one step at a time. You got this! One step at a time; you can handle anything.*

Doing research in 1992 wasn't easy, and even learning what the diagnosis meant was difficult because there were limited resources compared to today. I found most of my information in brick-and-mortar type places like the good old library and bookstores. Unlike today where I can get out my laptop and search the vast internet information highway, I had to get in my car and drive and obtain information from health care providers such as my gastroenterologist, my family doctor, and other specialists.

In my case, there wasn't a lot written about PBC because it is rare and usually only predominantly affects women aged 40 to 60. I was prescribed medication, however, the side effects scared me, so I took them but not as prescribed. I learned that there were important things I needed to know once I received my diagnosis. I had to discover imperative steps to comfort

Chapter 4

myself. I wanted to enjoy daily living as much as possible, so I found resources to help me make good decisions for myself and my future. Facing my diagnosis head-on was the best way to get through it and get better. Here is the medical definition: *The disease is called primary biliary cholangitis (PBC) because the immune system attacks the bile ducts inside the liver, which damages them. When immune cells surround and attack parts of the body, this is called inflammation. Inflammation of the bile ducts is called cholangitis. The medical term "primary" in this case means that there is no known reason for this damage to happen. Because the disease blocks or prevents the flow of bile, PBC is known as a "cholestatic" liver disease.*[10]

There are times when I perceived myself as if I was riding a bike, with the wind blowing through my hair, the sun shining down on my face, and birds singing. And then, Bam! I hit a bump out of the blue and find myself tits up, ass over tea kettle, flat on my back. As a result, the world as I see it may never look the same again. I assimilated that feeling when my doctor told me he was referring me to a gastroenterologist. Some of the questions that went through my mind were, *How will my life be different? Will I have a normal life?* I also wondered if I could do my job, take care of my kids, have a good relationship with my husband. And finally, I worried about how my friends and family might react, and even what my neighbours might think of me. LOL! I really did worry about that to some degree.

Initially, I was in shock, which triggered a flood of questions. Some of them were not very helpful. They didn't empower me to think about what I could do to make a difference or help me have confidence in my abilities. I needed to find an opportunity to see and act differently. I believe we all have an underlying

---

[10] Canadian Liver Foundation, liver.ca, Primary Biliary Cholangitis

attitude about life itself. Put another way, each one of us sees the world differently. For me, I have always perceived it as not that bad, given that I know others in much worse situations. As I mentioned, my reaction when receiving my diagnosis was that it was no big deal; I'm a long way from 60, and I don't appear to be sick. What I learned was more than half the people with PBC are diagnosed when blood tests are done for other reasons, such as routine testing, and there are usually no noticeable symptoms when diagnosed. There may be no symptoms for years during the early stages, and if treatment begins early, medication can slow its progression.

Health-wise, my life as I knew it pretty much carried on as usual, and I had no symptoms for years. Several months later, in January of 1994, my dad passed away in Edmonton, Alberta, and our family flew out to attend his funeral. I had committed to giving the eulogy, and although I developed laryngitis due to the change in weather, I kept my word. I have always been dependable and trustworthy and wouldn't let a little thing like laryngitis stop me. Five days later, we returned to Victoria, and I returned to work. I was at my desk the first morning when the director asked me for a file. It took me some time to find it, and I realized I had returned to work too soon. I'm guessing she saw this as unacceptable behavior because, the next thing I knew, I was relocated to a new desk, assigned new duties, and replaced by someone else.

I had so much shame, and I was angry, hurt, and frustrated and wanted to hide from the world. I tried to turn myself inside out in my mind while beating myself up for not being the person she needed me to be. Several people, courses, and books helped me change my thoughts and see things differently. One of the staff members told me anyone could take the Myers-Briggs Personality Type Test through work at no cost. The test helped me understand myself better, the people around me, and the director, who was still my boss even though I was no longer her administrative assistant.

Around this time, my husband enrolled in a Dale Carnegie Course,[11] a 12-week program that helped people speak in public with confidence. It was based on three books, *How to Win Friends and Influence People*, *How to Stop Worrying and Stop Living*, and *The Quick and Easy Way to Effective Speaking* all authored by Dale Carnegie. There was such a change in my husband that I knew I needed to enroll in the next available program. I gained so much confidence and self-awareness and was never the same at work again. It was a very proud moment when my husband, children, and several friends watched me receive the Highest Achievement Award, chosen by the program participants for the person they believed accomplished the most in the 12 weeks.

One of my friends and I worked together, and she attended my graduation. The next day, she sent out an email to the entire department, letting them know I had won this award. It was another time when I was proud of who I was and who I was becoming. Although I didn't work directly for the director again, there were a few occasions when our paths crossed, and my body became tense, my throat was dry, and anxiety washed over me. Several months later, I was in a bookstore, and the book *You Can Heal Your Life* by Louise Hay jumped off the shelf.

I acted on several suggestions in the book. One of the suggestions was to do mirror work, and the instructions were to stand in front of a mirror and have a conversation with someone who hurt you; no holding back, tell them exactly

---

[11] https://www.dalecarnegie.com/en

what is on your mind, swear words and all. It was awkward and embarrassing standing in front of the mirror the first time. I remember waiting until my kids were asleep and my husband was out before I had the courage to act. I stood in front of the mirror and pretended I was talking to the director; I unleashed all my emotions, and after doing this several times, I noticed a shift in my self-esteem.

I was at work several weeks later when I was asked to deliver a file to the director's office. From that day forward, I could pass her in the hall, be in the same meeting, or see her in the washroom, and I was delighted that I was at peace and confident. I knew I was no longer a victim. In fact, I reflected on the comment she made several years earlier when she said I was a square peg in a round hole, and I realized she had been a great teacher.

Chapter 4

My Recipe For So What!—Now What?

- *Learn from my children about coping with life;*
- *Follow the Kids Are Worth It—Six Critical Messages[12];*
- *Take a breath, one step at a time, I got this;*
- *Keep learning—When I know better, I do better;*
- *Be vulnerable, take risks, and do my work;*
- *Ask for help and support.*

My Self-Reflection

I believe my husband and I continued to change our past programming, behaviours, and beliefs, and that had a positive impact on our children. We did our best to model the behaviours we wanted our children to emulate. We believed we are our children's most significant influencers and teachers and knew they were watching and learning from us every day. We continued to keep our commitment to each other to spend some money on personal development, and we supported each other when faced with tough decisions.

---

[12] Ibid

What is Your Recipe For So What!—Now What?

Chapter 4

Given Your Recipe, Share Your Self-Reflection

V

There Are No Mistakes, Only Lessons

There are no mistakes in life, only lessons.
There is no such thing as a negative experience,
only opportunities to grow,
learn and advance along the road of self-mastery.
From struggle comes strength.
Even pain can be a wonderful teacher.

~ Robin Sharma

Several months after my father's funeral, I was moved to a different position where I utilized my newfound skills and abilities. It seemed easier to communicate with others, I was more confident to bring ideas to my new manager, and I was asked to create training manuals. I have since discovered that, before Dr. Janet G. Woititz published her book, *Adult Children of Alcoholics*, Tony A. published *The Laundry List in 1978*. This is not the entire list but the characteristics that resonate with me.

The Laundry List[13]

1. We became isolated and afraid of people and authority figures.
2. We are frightened by angry people and any personal criticism.
3. We live life from the viewpoint of victims, and we are attracted by that weakness in our love and friendship relationships.
4. We get guilt feelings when we stand up for ourselves instead of giving in to others.
5. We became addicted to excitement.
6. We have "stuffed" our feelings from our traumatic childhoods and have lost the ability to feel or express our feelings because it hurts so much (Denial).
7. We are dependent personalities who are terrified of abandonment and will do anything to hold on to a relationship in order not to experience painful abandonment feelings, which we received from living with sick people who were never there emotionally for us.
8. Alcoholism is a family disease; and we became para-alcoholics and took on the characteristics of that disease even though we did not pick up the drink.
9. Para-alcoholics are reactors rather than actors.

I mention this here because I perceived the director I worked for as an authority figure. I also recognized that I viewed myself as a victim and encountered feelings of guilt when standing up

---

[13] Tony A., Dan F., *The Laundry List*: The ACOA Experience, Health Communications, November 1, 1990

for myself. There were endless opportunities to be vulnerable, stretch my comfort zone, and take some risks. I co-facilitated a harassment workshop, a new initiative for employees that the organization rolled out. I was the treasurer of the social committee, within which I organized many events, including a Christmas dinner and dance gala attended by approximately 300 staff members and guests. I was vulnerable and courageous, taking on the master of ceremonies role. I may have thrown myself into these roles to create excitement. However, doing so took courage and gave me confidence.

I continued to look for opportunities to change my inner story—what I thought and believed. A friend I met through Beta Sigma Phi, a group of women who supported each other in many ways including having some fun, told me about a course her husband just finished taking. The course was called The Pursuit of Excellence, which was offered over five days in Vancouver, BC, by Context Associated. It sounded like the perfect next step, so I got approval from my employer to pay for the course and travel. Since I enrolled in the next scheduled program with my friend, I could stay with her and her husband.

The course changed my paradigm, believing that life happens for me, not to me. I was vulnerable and took a risk the first night volunteering to take on a leadership role. I had no idea what I was signing up for and found myself standing in front of a group of about 50 participants who expected me to take charge. I realized there were many times when I didn't listen to the rules, and this was one of them. Since I didn't know anyone, I was able to admit that I didn't listen to the rules and had no idea what I was doing. At the end of the exercise, the participants gave me a standing ovation, and I gained more confidence to stand out versus fitting in.

Working for BC System helped me recognize some of

the survival behaviours I learned as a child, growing up in a dysfunctional environment that no longer served me well. As I began to take on more leadership roles and change my thought patterns, I began thinking about a career change. Around the same time, a friend I hadn't heard from in years called to ask if I was open to exploring a different career option, and I gave her a resounding *Yes*. It was in the financial services industry with a multi-level marketing component.

I've since learned that my thought patterns can repeat themselves until I become fully aware of them, empowering me to make changes. For example, my husband and I were in the process of renovating our handyman special but didn't have the money, so we continued to charge our credit cards, as well as put a second mortgage on our house. By this time, my husband had finished his training at Camosun College and was offered an opportunity to go into business with three other partners. He was excited about being a co-owner of a technology company. Although we didn't have the money to invest in the business, we put a third mortgage on our house. We always had support from our family, and this time was no different with my husband's brother and a brother-in-law helping him purchase a more significant piece of the company. I recognized that we were continuing to make poor financial decisions.

Several months into the partnership, my husband discovered that his department was generating the most money, so he asked for a greater percentage of the profits. The partners disagreed and changed the locks on the doors overnight. I was still working for BC Systems while starting my training with the financial services company, and I was invited to attend a convention in Calgary. My husband wanted to support me with my career change, so he came along on the road trip. He attended one of the meetings and decided to join me in my venture since he was also looking for a different career. He studied, wrote the necessary exam, and passed with flying colours a week later.

I was devastated because, in my mind, he seemed to be better than me at everything. However, I didn't know how to express or stand up for myself, and I feared being abandoned by him if I did. I didn't recognize my fear of abandonment at the time and hung onto our relationship for dear life, and I'm not sorry I did. I compared my weaknesses to my husband's strengths. In fact, it wasn't only my husband who I compared myself to. I know I was insecure and feared failure, but I neglected to see my value in our relationship and this situation we found ourselves in.

I let my ego get in the way and didn't do enough research about the industry. It took me four attempts to pass the insurance exam, and I then realized this industry didn't play to my strengths. I might have kept my job if my husband hadn't written the exam and passed. I decided to leave to support my husband because we thought we could be successful as a team. BC Systems was simultaneously downsizing and offering severance packages to those who wanted to pursue other endeavours. I believed my husband, and I could create a client base and a team, and I had my severance to fall back on if we needed it.

We worked diligently together over the next few years to make this new career choice work. Since the industry was based on commission sales, we decided to sell our house because it became very challenging to manage our financial commitments. It was a blessing in many ways because we realized we were living someone else's life; neither one of us was interested in yard work or owning a fixer-upper.

When our children were old enough to understand, we

included them in decisions that impacted them, so we told them we were going to sell our house. When they were around ten and twelve, we began having family meetings and family nights. When we sold our house, we paid off all three mortgages and rented a house in the same neighborhood as our children's schools. We rented several places over the next few years, and it occurred to me that we were repeating a pattern from the '80s when our children were young; we were living like gypsies again.

We continued to invest in personal growth and purchased a cassette tape series, Personal Power by Tony Robbins. My greatest learning from this tape series was *The past does not equal the future.* Our takeaway was to keep acting on our goals because it's impossible to fail as long as we learned something from what we did. I've since learned that whenever I zero in on any aspect of myself that I want to change, my level of awareness heightens, so it seems that my circumstances worsen simply because I'm fully conscious of them. However, I've also learned that awareness can be the cure if I focus on what I want to change to dissolve old patterns. The process can be tricky because it's easy to think, *This technique is not working,* or *This is wasted effort because things seem to be getting even worse!* Master Sheng-Yen said, *Before you meet with success, failure is natural and necessary. As a baby learns to walk, it keeps falling down. Is this failure?*

While my husband was studying for his mutual funds' license, we decided to move and look for a cheaper house to rent because our monthly income was very low. We had the money for the damage deposit but not for the first month's rent. In this situation, I realized I could focus on my inside calm and visualize the outcome I wanted by not letting outside circumstances dictate my future. I believed strongly that I

Chapter 5

could sell our furniture and have enough money to cover the rent with money to spare. Someone called about our TV, and when I told her it had sold, she asked me if I had anything else for sale. I told her we had a Palliser bedroom suite I hadn't advertised yet, and she said one of her friends was looking for the same set. I told her the price, and her friend arrived the next morning with a truck and 1,000 dollars in cash. The Universe knew I needed to sell that bedroom suite and gave me a helping hand.

We lived in our next rental for several months, and even though it was less rent, we still struggled financially. I was collecting employment insurance as part of my severance package, but I had not yet received my severance payment. We pretty much lived on potatoes and had to give away our family dog. It was heartbreaking, but we found her a good home. Then one day, we got a call from my husband's brother and sister-in-law, who lived in Edmonton, saying they wanted to stop in Victoria for a visit on their way to Campbell River. The day we expected them, we didn't have a dime to our name, and our cupboards were bare. I did not have the courage to share our financial situation, with a visual of Old Mother Hubbard flashing before me. Once again, I knew I needed to trust the Universe, and I reminded myself to have faith and stay calm. They arrived while my husband and I were out at a meeting. So, they took our children out to the mall for lunch and bought a deck of cards. I checked our mailbox as soon as we arrived home, and there it was, a superannuation cheque for a few thousand dollars. *Thank you, thank you, thank you,* I said to the Universe. We immediately deposited the cheque, and I bought a ton of groceries, with our relatives having no idea at the time. I realize today that my teenage children may have been ashamed, and they may have also thought they had to keep the family secret about our financial situation. Thankfully, I continued the process of changing my thoughts and beliefs.

We were successful by many people's viewpoints because we had one of the largest teams in the office, and my husband won a trip. Our teenage children were excited to have their grandma stay with them while we were away on an all-expense-paid trip to San Francisco, including several dinners, hotel accommodation, and flights. The crazy thing was that we were faking it until we made it because we only had 67 dollars in our pockets for any meals not included and souvenirs for our children. It was also strange to be hobnobbing with financially successful people, staying in a five-star hotel, and eating fancy dinners at several banquets when we were broke.

Since my husband won the trip, and it was viewed as a level of success in the industry, I was asked to speak at one of our weekly meetings. I was excited but also embarrassed, and I now realize it was because I held the secret that we weren't making enough money to support our family, and I didn't want anyone to know that. I instantly understood that my mind was catapulted back to when I lied to my mother-in-law many years earlier. The memory of wanting to throw up from disgust and betrayal reminded me I wasn't living from a place of integrity. It wasn't congruent with how I wanted to live, and it didn't make sense to be excited about how we were making a living when we weren't even able to support our family.

We continued to model a strong work ethic, listen to motivational speakers, and believe in ourselves. Our children witnessed their parents' commitment to each other and to them, and I believe it had a positive impact. Evidence of this occurred when a friend of our son wanted to participate in some shenanigans. To his friend's surprise, our thirteen-year-old son said, *I never listen to anyone more messed up than me.* He had heard this from a cassette tape we had listened to hundreds of times. The series was *How to Master the Art of Selling* by Tom Hopkins. My son doesn't remember the incident as clearly as I do. However, he remembers us telling him how proud we were of him for standing up for himself.

We decided to make a consumer proposal because we found ourselves unable to meet our financial commitments again. Since we had already filed bankruptcy and a consumer proposal had less of a negative effect on our credit scores, it was our best option. As a parent of teenage children, it was very embarrassing to be in this financial position, having to seek professional help—again. When I look back at this time, I realize I was not thinking of the consequences of my decisions. I allowed my ego's desire *to be somebody* influence me throwing caution to the wind. I didn't know my definition of success, so I bought into the world's definition. Somehow, I believed hard work equalled success. What I didn't know was communicated by Yohnce Salimu, *Success is personal, so stop comparing your apples to their oranges.*

I had this perception that by middle age, I should have a successful career, well-adjusted polite teenagers, a perfect marriage, a beautiful home in a well-sought-after neighbourhood, a financial portfolio to die for, and the list goes on. So, I worked my fingers to the bone, and when our financial situation got worse, I worked even harder.

I realized I needed to earn some money to supplement our income because it was not consistent and didn't come in at the same time every month. I wanted daily cash, so I answered an ad for door-to-door canvassing. The volunteering I had done with my mom helped me find the courage to entertain this line of work. It was an extremely challenging way to make a few bucks, but it helped me put food on the table. In the beginning,

I wasn't very good at it, and many people yelled at me or slammed their door in my face. Shame and embarrassment washed over me, doing this kind of work at middle age.

The kind and compassionate lady who trained and supported me became a friend, and I stuck with it due to her belief and confidence in me. I could include my teenage children on a few occasions, so they witnessed their mom's determination and hard work. I met many wonderful people, learned a lot about myself, and gained some faith. My mom always believed in God and often recited the first line of Psalm 23. As I walked from one door to the other, I repeated these words, *The Lord is my Shepherd, I shall not want* over and over, and I believe it kept me safe from harm.

While living in Regina, our daughter took asthma medication through a nebulizer. However, when we found a doctor in Victoria, he prescribed several inhalers. We were grateful she didn't have to be on the nebulizer anymore and thought the climate on the West Coast may have helped. However, there were occasions when our daughter's asthma flared up, and our doctor prescribed medication. On one occasion, I couldn't afford to have the prescription filled immediately, but I knew I needed to have faith that I could earn the money that evening to pay for it the next day.

There had never been an evening that I earned the amount of money I needed for her prescription. But as I knocked on each door, I held the vision of picking up the prescription the next day and paying cash for it. I arrived at a townhouse, gained an instant rapport, and delivered my speech. A man opened his wallet and gave me every single dollar in it. I repeated the phrase from Psalm 23 in my mind as he handed me each bill. At the end of the evening, I had enough money to pay cash for the prescription.

Chapter 5

My husband and I believed we could create a lucrative income in this industry over time, and we worked diligently at it for four years. Neither of us had done any research to determine if we had the skills and abilities to do so, or whether we might love the process or the environment. Perhaps, it was a pipe dream. We made many friends, met wonderful people, and had tons of support from everyone we met. I often thought of the old Kenny Rogers' song, *The Gambler, You've got to know when to hold 'em, know when to fold 'em, know when to walk away and know when to run*. Perhaps we stayed in this industry a little too long. However, we did learn a lot about ourselves and how to get up, dust ourselves off, and keep learning and growing.

When we received an eviction notice on our townhouse door, the writing was on the wall; we could not go on living this way. Our 15-year-old son was the first to see it, and since it was our third notice, we had to move out by the end of the month. I was humiliated that he saw it first, and thoughts of remorse and disgust over our situation engulfed me. I realized I was repeating the enabling patterns of my mom. My husband and I knew we had to take some serious action, so we made an appointment with someone from the social assistance office to ask for financial help and support.

Sitting together in that office was not my husband's or my proudest moment. We had to explain why we were in such a financial mess. They agreed to help us if one of us was gainfully employed and earned a consistent income. They gave us a cheque to cover rent for two months and a few hundred dollars for groceries. This was one of the most devastating and stressful situations we had ever found ourselves in. I think the added pressure of being middle aged with teenage children made us think we should know better and do better. But we believed in each other, and together, we knew we could get through our challenge if we faced it head-on. My husband applied to Royal Roads University, and I took a term position with the provincial government.

I didn't easily express my emotions or talk about them with my children because I thought I had to be stoic and positive. I always included them in what was going on, and we had many conversations about our current situation. I often wonder if I squelched my emotions during my growing up years—shoved them under a rug, so to speak. I remember being told I was the oldest and had to set an example for my siblings. I was told to stop blubbering, *Grow up, Debra, and get on with it. We don't have time for that.* I believe I grew a very tough skin along the way and had to be strong for everyone else, so there was no time for crying or emotions. I became emotionally distant and learned to numb my feelings because people needed me to be strong; if I showed any emotion, I wasn't strong. Over the years, I have learned to open my heart, tap into my emotions, and label them. This is a daily work in progress, even now.

I read a book around this time entitled *If Life is a Game, These are the Rules* by Cheri Carter Scott, which included Ten Rules for Being Human. I treated the Rules like a recipe that really helped me move forward with confidence and deepened my commitment to my family and personal growth.

Ten Rules for Being Human[14]

1. You will receive a body
   You may love it or hate it, but this one body will be yours for the duration of your lifetime on earth.

---

[14] https://www.drcherie.com/ten-rules-for-being-human/

2. You will be presented with lessons
   You are enrolled in a full-time informal school called "life." Each day in this school you will have the opportunity to learn lessons. You may like the lessons or hate them, but you have designed them as part of your curriculum.
3. There are no mistakes, only lessons
   Growth is a process of trial and error: experimentation. The "failed" experiments are as much a part of the process as the experiment that ultimately "works."
4. A lesson is repeated until learned
   A lesson will be presented to you in various forms until you have learned it. When you have learned it, you can then go to the next lesson.
5. Learning does not end.
   There is no part of life that does not contain lessons. If you are alive, there are lessons to be learned.
6. *There* is no better than *here*.
   When you're *there* has become a *here*, you will simply obtain another *there* that will again, look better than *here*.
7. Others are only mirrors of you.
   You cannot love or hate something about another person unless it reflects to you something you love or hate about yourself. Each reflection is an opportunity for growth.
8. What you make of your life is up to you.
   You have all the tools and resources you need, what you make of them is up to you. The choice is yours.
9. Your answers lie inside you.
   The answers to life's questions lie inside you. All you need do is look, listen, and trust.

10. You will forget all this at birth.
Throughout the process of life, you will have opportunities to remember if you choose.

I memorized the rules, posted them on the fridge, and reflected on them often. They were a reminder to change my focus when old patterns of self-loathing and criticism crept back in.

The two rules I reflected on the most were the third, *There are no mistakes, only lessons.* And the fourth, *A lesson is repeated until learned.* Although I wasn't aware at the time, I have since learned that I was unconsciously demonstrating co-dependent behaviour. Codependency is a response to trauma, and as a child, I developed traits to deal with a chaotic and dysfunctional environment. I wanted to keep the family secret, so I couldn't tell people about our problems. As a result, I developed an unhealthy focus on other people's problems and needs. I was sensitive to criticism and beat myself up relentlessly.

Focusing on caring for others enabled me to wall off and deny my emotions. I recognized I had become a workaholic and often overextended myself. I didn't realize I was disconnected from my emotions, and therefore, I didn't know how to ask for what I needed. I bent over backwards to keep others and my family happy, and I stayed small and quiet to divert attention away from myself. I recognize now that my old pattern of locking myself into a course of action without accepting the possible consequences created inconsistencies and chaos for my family and me.

Many of the lessons I learned supported me not to be co-dependent, speak up for myself, and identify my self-worth. I quite often use the phrase up *until now*, which is a strong message to my mind that I no longer think or believe that

Chapter 5

thought or story. The shame and self-loathing are gone because I have learned to change my beliefs, stories, and family patterns. When I look back, I wonder why we made the decisions we did. On the other hand, I remind myself that we consciously modelled commitment, a strong work ethic, and resiliency. We listened to our children and trusted them to make their own choices. As a result, both of them had a healthy self-esteem as teenagers and didn't allow peer pressure to influence their decisions.

Proof of this occurred after our daughter's first few days at a new junior high school. She informed us that returning to that school or any other junior high school was not an option because it was an unhealthy environment for her to learn in. When we told her that quitting school was not an option, she replied, *If you and dad can choose the types of environments and people you want to associate with, then why can't I?* We began to witness her strong independent spirit more and more, and there were times when it was challenging to parent a child who knew who she was at such a young age. For example, when she was about fourteen, I remember telling her that she was picky. She replied, *Mother, I am not picky, I just know what I like.* And when I asked too many questions, she answered, *Mother, what's with the 50 questions?*

She always had an eye for fashion and developed her own website in the early '90s. She completed her junior and senior high program in a self-paced distance education system. She was always creative—drawing and painting, with an eye for colour and décor. She moved to Vancouver in her early 20s and earned her GED while working at Starbucks as a Supervisor. In the show Schitt's Creek, there is a line that the character Moira Rose says to the character Stevie Budd, *What the hell is your secret; you just stand your solid ground refusing to be anyone but you!* I could have said that about my daughter at any age or stage of her life, and I am proud and privileged to be her mother.

Where did I go wrong, or did I? I heard someone say once, *There are times when things will fall apart, so better things can fall together.* I know this to be true today. However, I figured I was a complete and utter failure before. My husband has said for years, *You cannot change one thing.* When something doesn't work out the way I plan, it doesn't mean I am a failure; if I learn something from it, it is part of life. What I learned was to believe in myself, and if I was calm on the inside, outside events didn't matter? I needed to trust in something outside of myself and let it go. Trusting the Universe was all about moving through my sinking feelings of doubt and fear and holding onto the belief that the Universe was handling the details. This wasn't always easy, and there are too many incidents to list that tested that trust.

I also learned that if things get worse initially, it's a great sign! It means whatever I'm doing is working, and I'm on the right path! Believe it or not, things are supposed to worsen before they get better. It seems counterintuitive, but I continue to look inward, learn to stand up for myself, and keep stepping up and showing up.

Chapter 5

My Recipe For Learning There Are No Mistakes, Only Lessons

- *Study the rules for being human;*
- *People will help people who are doing the best they know how;*
- *Get up after falling, and do what I can from where I am with what I have;*
- *Include age-appropriate children in my challenges;*
- *Stay calm on the inside, no matter what my outside circumstances are;*
- *Write my definition of success;*
- *Take responsibility for the role I play.*

My Self-Reflection

We grew stronger as a couple and a family because we believed in each other, never gave up, and had friends and family support. We always had someone help us move, give us a ride, lend us a car, invite us for dinner, or buy us groceries. People believed in us because we believed in ourselves, our family dynamics, and each other. I truly believe this was a time in our lives when things did fall apart so better things could fall together. We all learned valuable lessons, became stronger individuals, and developed a strong family bond.

What is Your Recipe For Learning There Are No Mistakes, Only Lessons?

Chapter 5

Given Your Recipe, Share Your Self-Reflection

VI

Recalibrating

If you don't ever find yourself recalibrating your decisions, you're likely ignoring some issues that might become problems down the line.

~ Carl Richards

Until now, my story may sound like I was struggling in many areas of my life and had no fun at all. I choose to view my journey as one that presented lessons until I learned them; they were part of my curriculum, and several lessons were repeated until learned. Throughout the rest of my memoir, I will introduce you to many people who helped me evolve, were with me during my transplants and recovery and helped me trust myself. In addition, I will include a few stories within which I trusted my intuition, used some tools from previous lessons, and practiced inner calm despite what was happening on the outside.

I often reflect on rule seven of the Rules for Being Human by Cheri Carter Scott, stating, *Others are only mirrors of you. You cannot love or hate something about another person unless it reflects to you something you love or hate about yourself. Each reflection is an opportunity for growth.*[15] I introduced you to my husband many chapters ago, and this rule often helped me in my relationship with him.

My husband has been one of my greatest teachers and rule seven helped me to view every interaction, communication, and argument with him as an opportunity for growth. As a result, I realized it was time to unlearn my co-dependant patterns and recognize behaviours and beliefs that did not work. There were times when my husband became angry, and my immediate response was thinking it was my fault, so I ran to see what I had done wrong, so I could fix it. Then, several years ago, I realized it wasn't my stuff; I needed to lay it down and let it go. I demonstrated an old behaviour pattern in our relationship and needed to let my husband work it out for himself.

In 1999, my husband enrolled in the Microsoft Certified Systems Engineer Program offered at Royal Roads University. We were grateful to have received grants and funding due to the age of our children and our financial situation. My husband suggested I investigate the degree programs at RRU because he wanted to support me to make a successful career change.

I continued working on my inner self-talk and started believing I could earn a University Degree. In 2001, at the age of 47, I enrolled as a mature student in their BCom Entrepreneurial Management program. I was excited and overwhelmed all at the same time because I knew I needed to leave my old thought of being stupid behind. I was not the same person who got Cs and Ds in school, and I reminded myself I had earned a Secretarial Certificate from the Northern Alberta Institute of Technology in 1974 and had developed

---

[15] www.mamasformamas.org/

Chapter 6

many other skills and abilities through work and raising a family. Through this process, there were several incidents that provided opportunities for me to act maturely and face my shortcomings. When I submitted my application to RRU, I was working for the provincial government and planned to continue working there until I finished the two-year program. The province's premier had other plans, making changes that affected my work hours, so I chose to take what they called a voluntary departure to ensure I could finish my degree. I discovered that it is not what happens to me, but how I choose to respond or react.

While on employment insurance, I applied for a position with the Federal Government and was called to take a clerical test. The test was scheduled for the same day as the final exam of one of my courses. I set a boundary and asked the examiner to reschedule my test. I was relieved I had the strength to be vulnerable and stand up for myself. And I was proud that I handled this situation in a mature fashion by not blaming anyone or acting like a victim. This was my curriculum and my lesson.

I continued seeing my gastroenterologist during my degree program, and on one of my visits, he seemed puzzled about my blood work and sent me for some additional tests. I was surprised when he told me I had celiac disease. I heard my mom's voice saying, *You have celiac*. Growing up, I had the belief that if I received a diagnosis of some sort, I should be sick. Since I did not follow a gluten-free diet and had no symptoms, I believed I outgrew it. I replied to the doctor, *I know I have celiac because I was born with it and outgrew it*. He shook his head in disbelief, *You don't outgrow celiac, and you need to go on an extremely strict gluten-free diet, or you are going to fade away to nothing.*

It turns out I never followed a completely gluten-free

diet until the day after I sat in my specialist's office. When I look back, it was a miracle that I successfully conceived and delivered two healthy children in the early 80s. I read every book on celiac and did some online research. I learned to read labels, what cross-contamination was, and how to cook gluten-free meals. This was another area where I discovered some old behaviour patterns and beliefs. As a result, I needed to speak up, set boundaries, and inform friends and family about what I could and could not eat. One of my old beliefs was that you are grateful for and eat what is put in front of you. It was my life and time to start setting healthy boundaries while letting go of any guilt for voicing my truth.

After the age of 20, there is a 34 percent chance of developing another autoimmune disorder when diagnosed with celiac. Because I believed I outgrew it and did not follow a gluten-free diet, it increased my risk of developing a second autoimmune disorder. I realized that the phrase, *What you don't know won't hurt you* wasn't true because I was oblivious to how celiac was harming my body.

Although earning a Bachelor of Commerce Degree in Entrepreneurial Management at night was challenging, because the learning curve was steep and the workload was enormous, I continued to make better decisions, set boundaries, and developed a sense of self-worth. In the final year of studying for my degree, the classes increased from two nights per week to four, and our team had an entrepreneurial project to complete. It was hair-raising! It was as if I was living my life at Mach 2 with my hair on fire. Nevertheless, our team knocked it out of the park with an A on our project. It was the first A I ever received and is one of my proudest moments to this day.

The night of our final class, I ran out of the building and, at the top of my lungs, yelled, *Yahoo!* With determination and the help and support from my teammates, many students, and my teachers, I, Debra Rachar, earned a Bachelor of Commerce Degree in Entrepreneurial Management. It was one of the most challenging and rewarding two years of my life, but I did it and took pride in who I was becoming. Walking across the graduation stage, receiving my degree in front of my children, my husband, and friends was worth attending every team meeting, writing, and rewriting every paper and taking every single exam. It was worth every late night and every stale muffin and cold cup of coffee.

Along the way, there were defining moments when I began shifting my thinking, changing my subconscious thoughts, and choosing more deliberate thinking over default thinking. I shifted old patterns of thinking and beliefs enough to be confident enough to earn a degree. That achievement gave me even more confidence, and I no longer believed I was stupid. I faced my challenges and became stronger, physically, mentally, and spiritually. Little did I know what a difference it would make 13 years later when I was lying in a hospital bed fighting for my life.

While in the final six months of my degree, a higher, more permanent position was posted with the Federal Government, and I decided to apply. I was learning from morning till night, and I thought my brain might shut down from exhaustion. However, I made it through those two years with the support of my classmates, co-workers, trainers, and team leader. I have since learned that adult children of alcoholics also possess positive characteristics, including resilience, maturity, responsibility, sensitivity, and they are driven.

I was very grateful for my husband's support while earning

my degree because there were several times when he needed to step in and deliver tough love with our young adult children. I needed to focus on my studies and learn a new job, and I could count on my husband to handle these situations. Receiving support from others when we needed it the most was also greatly appreciated.

The unlearning of co-dependant patterns may be lifelong for me, but several occurrences before and after my liver transplants are worth mentioning. Our children were mostly working and living independently after my husband and I achieved our perspective certificate and degree. I suddenly observed that I viewed my husband as an authority figure and was afraid to stand up for myself. Reminding myself of lesson four of the rules for being human—*A lesson is repeated until learned*[16]—I saw that the area I seemed to struggle with the most was finances. One of the reasons we had challenges was that I had a poor relationship with money and could not express my thoughts and emotions around the subject.

For my husband and me, it seemed our lesson had to do with how each of us regarded money and how we individually managed it. I must admit, I had the ostrich syndrome, just wanting to bury my head in the sand and not handle it. I didn't want any more confrontations, plus I didn't know how to communicate effectively to prevent them.

Through my husband's financial-services encounter, he discovered he was better suited as an entrepreneur and went into business for himself. He also worked part-time for the school board as a computer technician to supplement our income while getting his business off the ground. In his spare time, he loved rebuilding motors and began the process of

---

[16] Ibid

Chapter 6

building a 1998 station wagon into a sleeper car. He came up with the crazy idea of purchasing a shipping container to place in our rental house driveway for somewhere dry to work on his car.

I knew this was a very irresponsible way to spend thousands of dollars and realized I needed to get my head out of the sand. I also wanted to start planning for retirement, get out of the rental market, and find an affordable living situation for our golden years. My thinking was that if we could find something we could afford to buy with a mortgage payment equal to our rent, we might be ahead of the game for once in our married life.

I began looking for a mobile home that we could qualify for based on my income since my husband had just started his business. Thankfully, my sister was able to help us with the down payment. In 2005 we found a mobile home with an attached garage, room to run a home-based business, and an amazing view of Brentwood Bay. In fact, I think we got a million-dollar view without the million-dollar price.

After learning that staying calm on the inside, no matter what my outside circumstances look like, I had many opportunities to practice my new-found knowledge, and it made such a difference in my relationship with others. One time that stands out was when my daughter was looking for a roommate, so she could afford to move back to Vancouver. Her dad and I loaded all her worldly possessions on our truck and were surprised when we arrived at the apartment building to learn that her new roommate was out of town. Our daughter told us her roommate had arranged for a friend to meet us at the building with the keys. We were parked in a narrow back alley, and the first series of thoughts that went through my mind were, *OMG, this person has taken my daughter's money and skipped town; what are we going to do with all her possessions on the truck now; she will never find another shared accommodation in one day, and she doesn't have the money.* Then I slowed down, reminding myself, *Woah, you're jumping to conclusions.* Fortunately, I knew my children could tell when their mother was freaking out on the inside, and I knew my daughter didn't need any more stress.

I chose to change my thoughts immediately and reminded myself that outside circumstances were no match for inside calm. I focused on a positive outcome, visualizing us unloading her belongings into her new apartment; I knew I needed to trust the Universe. We waited in the back alley for about an hour when the roommate's friend showed up with the keys. It was one of the first times I recognized that my energy, thoughts, and beliefs could have a positive or negative outcome in any situation. It taught me that my old patterns of thinking and fear dominated my mind at first, but I could remain calm, visualize a positive outcome, and let the Universe handle the details.

Due to living in a different province from most of our family, we could not always attend our nieces' and nephews' weddings. However, one of our nieces had a destination wedding in Mexico a few years after we moved into our mobile home, and my husband and I were excited to be able to attend and stay at an all-inclusive resort for the first time. It was a fabulous trip and a great time spent with our family, including the honour of witnessing our niece's wedding.

I worked for the pension department for several years and chose to apply for several promotions. However, after not getting the job several times, I decided to improve my communication skills. One of my co-workers recently joined a Toastmasters club, and I learned that their agenda included a Table Topics session. Toastmaster members and guests are called upon and given a topic to speak about for a minimum of one minute. I knew Toastmasters could help me gain more confidence during the interview process and assist in advancing my career.

I found a club that fit my schedule, held many positions on the executive, competed in speech contests, was the chair for several speech contests, and met some amazing people from all walks of life. I also made a few lifelong friends. I was proud of my achievements and disappointed when I had to leave due to primary biliary cholangitis symptoms. The skills I learned at Toastmasters greatly improved my ability to write government exams and think on my feet during the interview process.

The next higher-level position that was posted required the university degree equivalent I had spent the time and money to earn several years earlier. It involved a nine-month training period that included learning policies, procedures, and legislation well enough to process applications for Canadian pensioners and solve complex problems. I found the learning curve steep, and I recalled the same sense of feeling overwhelmed that I experienced while studying for my degree. The most challenging requirement for me was to be both accurate and fast. It didn't help that I compared myself to other trainees who understood the material the way it was taught. Fortunately, as trainees, we had staff designated to verify our work. In addition, we were also assigned a coach to help us manage our workload, answer questions, and confirm our decisions.

A pivotal point in my training was when I wasn't sure if I was meeting the standard requirements for trainees. My coach and many of my team members helped and supported me to get through my training and embrace my learning curve. However, even though I had help and support, I continued to struggle with the amount of information I needed to retain regarding policies, procedures, and legislation. There was an enormous amount of work, and we were expected to produce a certain amount every day. Since my speed and accuracy weren't up to par, my team leader asked me what I wanted to do? I told her I was open to her suggestions. So, she decided to organize my workload, instructing me what to work on each day, and she advised me not to talk to anyone. I was extremely embarrassed and ashamed, but I held my head high, reflected on my inner calm, and with the help of my teammates, I made it through the steep learning curve. My commitment to finishing what I start, learning from my mistakes, and trusting my teammates helped me believe in myself.

A few years after we moved into our mobile home, I had another opportunity to voice my truth and set good boundaries. My husband was having his own health issues and not sleeping well due to sleep apnea. He wasn't diagnosed yet and wasn't thinking clearly. He suggested we sell and move back to Alberta because he thought we could help his aging parents, and he could start a business there. Many extended family members lived in Alberta, and he thought he could help them by using his expertise in the technology industry. We had both just turned fifty-two, and there was no way in hell I was going to start over again. My days for living like a gypsy were over—been there done that, got too many t-shirts to count. The boundary I set was that if he wanted to move and start a business in Alberta, I could join him once he was well established and making a substantial income. I was so proud of myself because I recognized I no longer had co-dependent behaviours, was not afraid to speak my truth, and set boundaries for how I wanted to live. Once he was diagnosed with sleep apnea, using a CPAP machine, and sleeping better, he realized it wasn't a good decision, so he decided to stay and work on the business he was already building.

Many years went by, and it seemed like nothing changed in terms of my health. I stuck to a celiac diet and took my medication sporadically. My first introduction to the liver transplant clinic was in 2009. We went over to Vancouver to see a liver transplant specialist. This was new territory for us, and we didn't plan it well. We didn't research the parking in the area or the length of time it took to get from one place to another. We must have appeared like hicks from the sticks. This incident helped us be more aware and prepared for future trips to Vancouver.

Since PBC progresses very slowly, I was scheduled for yearly check-ups at the transplant clinic. If you are navigating your diagnosis and possible surgery, please do your homework and find out what financial resources might be available. We paid for our transportation for appointments to the liver transplant clinic before we realized there were provincial resources to help families with travel costs for medical appointments.

Since we continued to receive family support, we wanted to reciprocate and support them whenever possible. As I became more aware of my thoughts, beliefs, and behaviours, I became more authentic by trusting myself and listening to my intuition. When I was in my early 50s, I listened to my intuition and joined my two sisters-in-law in Alberta to declutter my mother-in-law's home. My mother-in-law always had a huge impact on my life and was there for me through thick and thin. I knew it was my turn to be there for her.

My son, who was working in Northern Alberta, heard about our decluttering project and came to help. There were a lot of emotions, tons of work, and many happy family memories made that weekend—one of the fondest involved my son and my mother-in-law. He and I removed canning jars from the cellar and hauled them down to the garden to dispose of their contents. My mother-in-law wanted to help empty the jars, and it was a beautiful spring day in May, so the three of us enjoyed connecting while soaking up the sun. As we emptied jar after jar, it became obvious that the garden was becoming a disgusting mess. At one point, my son opened a jar that sort of exploded all over him. We thought it was apple juice, but he said, *I feel like I just peed myself.* We all had a good howl. Then my mother-in-law retorted, *Can you imagine if anyone was driving by right now and saw us and the contents of the garden? They might think, oh, those poor people; they must be so sick.* We all burst out in hysterical laughter, and my mother-in-law laughed so hard she fell over into the dirt, and I thought I was going to pee myself.

My mother-in-law was very supportive, a good friend, and the best grandmother to our children. She was there for our family in our darkest hours, and always had time for everyone. She always had the kettle on for tea and a pie or cake to serve along with it. She loved babies and children, and she was often found reading a story to a child sitting on her lap. When she passed away several years later, and even now, I think back to how proud I am of who she was, who I was, and who the three of us were together that sunny spring day, laughing hysterically at ourselves. We were grateful that my daughter, her fiancé, and our son were able to attend her funeral, and although she wasn't living when I had my liver transplants, she was in my heart every step of the way.

One of the characteristics I developed as an adult child of an alcoholic was difficulty having fun. I was well into my fifties and completely unaware I was so serious; I had no idea how to

Chapter 6

have fun. At one point, I was taking an out-of-town workshop and had to answer some questions before attending. One of the questions was, *What do you do for play?* I honestly didn't know how to answer the question, so I showed the question to my husband. He said, *Play? You don't play.* I thought, *Oh, my, I need to let my guard down and allow my spunky self to be seen and heard.* The awareness that I took life too seriously made me realize that it's never too late to lighten up.

I have one friend who I seem to connect with in a different way, one who inspired me to set bigger goals and encouraged me to dream bigger. She challenged me to take a leap of faith. I never anticipated meeting her, and recognizing she was unique didn't occur to me immediately. I met this unique woman while driving to a convention, and when we arrived in the wee hours of the morning, we discovered we were sharing a bed. It's kind of fun when people ask how we met because we say, *Oh, we slept together.* We had an instant connection and became friends immediately. Since then, we meet weekly and continue to discuss our goals and dreams, how we want to show up in the world, and how we can support each other. My friend attended a conference and heard a speech by Sharon Wood, who was the first Canadian Women to summit Everest. We began to explore the idea of calling our weekly connections *The Climb*.

Over the last ten years, *The Climb* has been a journey to support and witness each other's wins and challenges and listen, help, and create space to grieve a loss or celebrate a victory. Hearing the words, *I see you* from someone else when you don't know or trust yourself is like having a lifeline, a cheerleader, and a coach at your fingertips. The intention was to support each other every step of the way as we climbed toward our summit of becoming the best versions of ourselves. Over time, we began asking ourselves and each other some questions,

What do we take with us? What do we leave behind? How do we want to show up in life for ourselves and others? After climbing together for several years, I often ask her how she is, and she replies, saying, *I'm living the dream.* And when she asks me how I am, I reply, saying, *I'm loving the adventure.*

My friend also helped me learn to lighten up and have fun because she's a travel agent and helped me and others by asking us this thought-provoking question, If you could take a trip anywhere in the world, where would you go? When it came to travel, my family and I usually visited our family. One trip was forever etched in my mind when my mother and father-in-law celebrated their 50th wedding anniversary. The family planned a houseboat trip on Shuswap Lake in the Okanagan. We rented three houseboats and had an absolute blast tubing, water skiing, hiking, and sitting around the campfires at night telling stories.

My friend created a women's travel meetup group, and I decided to join, and she asked me that question, *If you could take a trip anywhere in the world, where would you go?* I realized I had never entertained the idea of taking a trip without my husband. The question helped me recognize that I had an old belief pattern that if my husband didn't want to travel, I shouldn't want to travel either. Since my friend was always talking about travel, she helped me believe I could start visualizing going on a trip with her. She and several friends were planning a trip with G Adventures, and I began dreaming of the possibility of being on this trip with them.

Several months later, my friend and I were in our room in a villa in Italy, standing at a window looking out over the Amalfi Coast with tears streaming down our faces. As we stood there drinking in the view, we were, in fact, *living the dream* and *loving the adventure.* We took several other life-altering trips together. She continues to be my climbing partner, who helped me lighten up, helped me believe I could travel without my husband, and still supports me in every way possible to be the best version of myself.

When I was about 22, I purchased a fridge magnet that reads, *I like my bifocals; my dentures fit me fine; my hearing aid is perfect; but Lord, I miss my mind.* I didn't quite picture myself wearing bifocals, dentures or hearing aids when I purchased it. However, even to this day, every time I read it, it makes me laugh. What I find particularly funny is the phrase, *Lord, I miss my mind.* As a young adult, I certainly did not have any appreciation about where my mind could have gone.

Fast forward some 40-odd years, I still find this portion of the phrase funny and have a sincere appreciation for how important it is to take care of my mind. Another spiritual teacher I have been studying for several years is Mike Dooley. His teachings contain the premise that our *thoughts become things.* I now understand that thoughts do become things, and that it is important to notice my thoughts is a way that develops a healthy mind. I have implemented a daily practice of meditation, reading, fresh air, and exercise. Every day, I am grateful for the opportunity to choose good thoughts and meditate on all the good in the world. There is a saying, *If you don't use it, you lose it.* Every day, I ask myself, *What can I do to sharpen my mind, to protect it from negative energy, and how can I inspire those around me?*

My Recipe For Recalibrating

- *The past does not equal the future;*
- *It's not what happens to me, it's how I respond or react to it;*
- *Lessons will be repeated until learned;*
- *Others are mirrors of me;*
- *Take care of my mind because losing it is not an option;*
- *Lighten up and have fun;*
- *Relationships change my perspective and help me grow;*
- *Set boundaries by communicating clearly what is okay with me and what isn't.*

My Self-Reflection

When I started to change old belief patterns, behaviours, and stories, my life improved in so many ways. I could finally voice my truth, set boundaries, and become less critical of myself. I recognized I was resilient, mature, responsible, and driven to become a better version of myself. I was no longer afraid of authority figures, and as I became more authentic, I no longer needed to depend on others to tell me who I was. I now choose relationships that inspire me to leave the drama and negative patterns behind.

Chapter 6

What is Your Recipe For Recalibrating?

Given Your Recipe, Share Your Self-Reflection

VII

Navigating Life With Symptoms

Health is relative. There is no such thing as an absolute state of health or sickness. Everyone's physical, mental, and emotional condition is a combination of both.

~ *Theodore Isaac Rubin*

Life came to a grinding halt for me for several weeks when my doctor diagnosed me with shingles in 2013. He indicated stress can cause shingles, and I thought, *stress? I don't have any stress.* I was in BIG TIME denial. I didn't realize that I associated stress with learned stress, such as financial, learning curve, or parenting stress. I wasn't aware that the single biggest cause of excessive stress is a lifestyle void of adequate physical and mental rest.

    I realized I was a people pleaser and still in the learning stages of how to set boundaries. The belief I had growing up of being lazy wasn't completely gone, and I was overcommitting and saying *yes* to everyone. I wanted to be liked, didn't want to let anyone down, and didn't realize I was seeking ways to be useful to others. I worked full-time as a public servant in a very fast-paced, high-volume work environment and had just started a network marketing business. I was also the bookkeeper for my husband's business, the president of my Toastmasters' Club, the telephone coordinator for a municipal counsellor's campaign, and the volunteer coordinator for the annual Christmas Spirit Community dinner. The latter was an event that fed over 1000 guests and provided Christmas gifts for all the children. I was running myself ragged.

One day, I was sitting at my desk, and my back started to hurt. I immediately dismissed it as a consequence of sitting funny. The next morning, my husband showed me pictures of my back that he had taken the night before. He asked me to promise to see a doctor before heading off for the weekend to a network marketing convention. I had committed to drive several people, and I was more committed to keeping my promise with them than taking the time to slow down, breath, and take my health seriously.

When I returned from the conference, I went to the doctor, and he gave me a note to stay off work for several weeks. But for some reason, my mind didn't want to stop, and I continued to work from home. I literally could not get out of bed a few days later, and I think my body said, *Enough is enough, if you aren't going to stop, I'm going to stop you!*

A speech contest was coming up in our Toastmaster Club, and I decided to deliver one entitled *Put Your Oxygen Mask on First*. While researching, I found an article in the February 12, 2014, issue of Psychology Today. The writer explains that if you grew up in an environment where your emotional needs were not met, or you were the primary caregiver for your parents instead of the other way around, you likely learned to be co-dependent—taking care of others and not taking care of yourself. Children often get the message growing up that putting themselves first is being selfish or, put another way, it is better to give than to receive. I grew up hearing these messages in an environment where I took on the role of co-parent most of the time.

I thought about the safety instruction I received every time I took a trip on a plane. In the case of an emergency, put your oxygen mask on first, and then assist your child or others. There is a reason they tell us this—we're not going to be much help to anyone if we're passed out or dead. I learned from contracting shingles that putting my oxygen mask on in my day-to-day life was equally if not more important than taking care of others. I have two questions I now ask myself to be sure I'm putting self-care first:

1. Am I saying No to me by saying *Yes* to you?
2. What one activity can I let go of that drains my energy?

I am very grateful I contracted shingles prior to having any symptoms from primary biliary cholangitis. It taught me that taking care of myself was imperative to maintain the strength I would need in the coming years.

In 2013, I received a small inheritance from my mom and invested the money in additional personal development. I enrolled in several courses in transformational education with Excellence Seminars International. The courses were life-changing and life-enhancing, which enabled me to uncover some additional beliefs that no longer worked for me.

One belief was that I was not good enough at some level in my relationship with my husband, my role as a parent, and my career. These courses helped me uncover that I heard criticism and the words *you're not good enough* whenever I received feedback from others. In this environment, I had the opportunity to become aware of this belief pattern and chose not to listen to my denigrating self-talk. Instead, I continued to work through my old beliefs and stories. When I recognized where the messages came from, I could ask myself if they were true, and because they weren't, I could let them go. It was an old belief that no longer served me, and I had gained more tools to empower and belief in myself.

The closer I got to age 60, the more curious I became about primary biliary cholangitis. To gain more information, I began to research sites like WebMD, the Canadian Liver Association, and others. What I learned was that I could do too much research while becoming fearful of the unknown and what might be looming around the corner. I wondered how my life was going to unfold. I also learned that, for me, it was a balance between not knowing and knowing what to expect. But I also noticed doing too much research caused anxiety and became overwhelming. Once I started visiting the transplant clinic, I received all the information, resources, and support I needed.

2014 was an epic year when our daughter got married in Vegas. It was a fabulous destination wedding, with many relatives attending. I was proud and privileged to speak at her wedding about her growing up and the life partner she chose. I knew she found her soulmate when my future son-in-law sent me a photo of a picture my daughter had painted for him to hang on his wall at work. She had dated many fellas and had lost or hid her creative side somewhere along the way. So, I was overjoyed she found someone she trusted to be her authentic self with.

Several months later, I travelled to Italy with a group of ladies on a G-Adventure tour. It was a trip of a lifetime and a vacation I will never forget. My friend was a travel agent and organized an excursion for several women to take a Caribbean cruise with Oceania cruise lines in December of that year, and she asked me to come along. My sister was turning 50, so she and I decided to jump on board and share a cabin.

My sister's daughter and I were very close, and she visited my husband and me frequently throughout her young life. She visited us for Christmas in 2014, two weeks after I returned from my cruise. On Christmas day, my niece and I were sitting in my truck, and she read the story, *The Brave Little Owl*, with her owl puppet performing the actions. We delivered hot chocolate to the homeless on the streets of downtown Victoria the same afternoon, and we were both in our element, enjoying every minute. I will cherish these memories of my niece and me in my heart forever. She was scheduled to fly home on December 26th, the same day our family celebrated Christmas that year. We had just finished dinner, and I was torn between driving my niece to the airport and leaving my family. I was reminded of a Ram Daas quote, *Be Here Now*. As she and I sat waiting for her flight, a thought crossed my mind, *Enjoy every second you have with her because you may not see her again*. I'm grateful I was present at the moment and hugged her with all my heart as if it might be our last—and it was.

My niece had the biggest heart of anyone I have known. She could always be found helping the homeless in whatever city she found herself living in. Her funeral was a very tragic and traumatic event for our family because she took her life at the young age of 22. She had a mental health illness, was diagnosed with depression, and took medication. I can only imagine the great emotional pain and loss of hope she must have been experiencing and, therefore, saw no other way to relieve her inner turmoil other than ending her life. *Rest in peace, my Brave Little Owl!*

I noticed I didn't cry at funerals and was certain everyone else did. I judged myself harshly and believed people thought I didn't care about the person who passed away. Since there was no way I could make myself cry, I decided to accept myself and realized everyone grieves differently.

Through my research of adult children of alcoholics, I learned that my emotional needs were not met due to inconsistency, unreliability, and environmental chaos growing up. I realized I denied my feelings of sadness, fear, and anger to survive. I had low self-esteem for many years, suppressed my emotions and lost my ability to label them. I learned these behaviours and coping skills as a child, and although I'm a work in progress, I can now face the issues and tap into my emotions while labelling them as they arise.

When my husband and I arrived at the transplant clinic in May 2015, we believed it was a routine appointment. We were expecting to hear what we had in previous appointments, which was that I had a Model for End-Stage liver Disease—MELD—score of seven, so they might see me in a year. A MELD score is a method used for transplant planning, and this time, they told us my score was twelve. We were scheduled to see a sociologist, psychologist, nurse, dietician, and surgeon. The higher and faster the score climbs, the closer you are to needing a transplant. This was the first time we saw a transplant surgeon, and he explained what to expect with a primary biliary cholangitis diagnosis. The liver could fail gradually over many years until it got to its final stage, and then one day, it could stop working, shut down, and it might seem to me like I'd been dropped off the end of a cliff! The transplant team provided us with all the details and next steps. After returning from our trip, my husband and I were standing in our kitchen, and my husband said, *I don't think the two people who went to the transplant clinic yesterday are the same two people standing here today.* Without thinking, the first three words out of my mouth were *Surprise, Surprise, Surprise*, in the voice of Jim Nabors, who played Gomer Pyle in the old TV series.

Everyone encounters a surprise at some point, gets thrown a curve ball, or receives an unexpected circumstance. Any one of these can be experienced at different times—an eviction notice on the door, the death of a loved one, being labelled a square peg in a round hole, receiving a diagnosis, or managing a pandemic, to name a few. How I respond to the events I am given is my choice, and I have recognized that one of my default responses to unexpected events is to become overwhelmed. I've learned to process what I'm feeling through journaling, and then share it with someone as soon as I can. I gathered the information I was given by the transplant team and began to move forward. I educated myself by researching the information I needed.

We required accommodations in Vancouver for up to three months after the transplant. We also needed at least 10,000 dollars for living expenses and support from friends and family who could help me once I was discharged from the hospital. I collected the forms I needed and talked to people about what I could put in place to prepare for the surgery. I read many articles on liver transplants, educated myself on terminology, and phoned people about possible accommodations. I did this about a year before the surgery. I was ready—*bring it on*. Or was I ready? I realized I wasn't because I took no action to create a financial plan for several months.

The day after the appointment, I recognized I had some fear, and some questions were running around in my head. How can I afford to be off work? Am I healthy enough to survive a major operation like this? What I learned was that being proactive calmed my fears. One phone call can make all the difference in reducing my anxiety and worry. A few months after the appointment, the common symptoms showed up. The three major ones are pruritus, confusion, and ascites.

I used to be one of those people everyone envied—the type whose head hits the pillow and doesn't hear a thing until they wake up. In fact, I slept so soundly that when I was on a cruise ship in April 2015, I didn't even hear a helicopter hovering over the vessel to load a passenger who needed medical attention. But that all changed when I found myself lying awake unable to fall asleep due to pruritus. Pruritus is a potentially incapacitating symptom caused by intense and unrelenting itching of the skin. It can affect one's quality of life and lead to severe fatigue, sleep disturbance, depression, and suicidal tendencies. The crazy thing is that, for me, it usually occurred in the evening and continued all night. I was going stark raving mad because there was no relief from the itching. And when I finally did get to sleep, the itching returned within an hour or two. This went on for several months and looking back, I don't know how I simultaneously held down a full-time job.

There are numerous tips and suggestions that support anyone to sleep better. Some did not work for me at all. My solution was to talk to everyone I knew about my situation, including my doctor, who didn't want to prescribe medication. However, some of the remedies, such as listening to music or reading a novel, worked some of the time. One suggestion I received from a friend was aromatherapy, and it worked the best. I bought some lavender oil and put it on a handkerchief on my pillow, and it worked most of the time. Since I became *Sleepless in Victoria*, I gained a new appreciation for people who are sleep-deprived, and I am grateful I talked to everyone I knew and had people who supported me.

During the summer of 2015, my husband and I thought a family vacation might help take my mind off the itching and provide a form of distraction. We stayed with some family members who frequently rented a cabin on a lake in Windemere, BC. The intention was to enjoy some summer fun like water skiing, tubing, and swimming. The weather had other plans that year, and it rained most of the time. As for the family vacation being a distraction from the itching, that really didn't happen, and I became distant because I was not my usual self and couldn't connect with those around me. Through my challenges, I discovered that the beautiful thing about spending time with my family is that they love and support me no matter what I'm going through. I thought I must have looked like a dog with fleas because I couldn't sit still and couldn't stop scratching.

I returned to work after our vacation, and a particular discussion took place regarding a specific type of work in a team meeting led by the team leader. Listening to Brené Brown speak about shame and vulnerability inspired me to admit out loud to the group that I had no idea what I was doing within this type of work. After the words came out of my mouth, I stopped breathing and waited for the shoe to drop. My inner voice said, *What the hell have I done; I could lose my job.* Fortunately for me, it was the right thing to do because I had a meeting with a different team leader and a manager several months later. They told me that management had dropped the ball, and I didn't have to do this type of work anymore. Thank you, Brené Brown.

Daring greatly means the courage to be vulnerable.
It means to show up and be seen.
To ask for what you need, to talk about how you're feeling,
to have the hard conversations.

~Brené Brown.

We were back at the transplant clinic in Vancouver a month after our family vacation, and they prescribed a medication that helped get the itching under control. How do you spell relief? No Itching and drugs! All the lessons I learned through work and the process of navigating symptoms of primary biliary cholangitis supported me to act maturely and no longer react negatively. On this visit, I expected to be told that my name was added to the transplant list—not this time. As I left their office, I was reminded of Henry Cooke's quote, *Life is what happens when you're busy making other plans.*

I was aware I was making plans in my mind for the next phase of my journey towards a liver transplant because at a previous appointment, a doctor told me that my name might be added to the list. I learned that just because someone tells you something, even if they are a professional, that doesn't make it real. What is real is how I think and act every moment of every day. I reflected on aspects of health and healing and wrote the following on September 20, 2015.

My Ten Mantras for a Journey to Optimal Health

1. I will be blessed beyond belief for all the miracles that are about to take place;
2. May all beings be filled with gratitude and joy on this journey;
3. The right people, at the right time, and in the right place will be inspired to use their gifts of healing;
4. My environment is always peaceful, beautiful, and nurturing;
5. My body is vibrant and heals easily and effortlessly;
6. I radiate positive light and goodwill along my path;

7. I live in Easy World[17] Breathe, Relax, Allow, and Enjoy;
8. I trust and listen to the voice within;
9. I allow the currents of abundance, love, and friendships to lift me higher;
10. Love, light, and healing illuminate from my spirit, body, and soul.

In December 2015, my gastroenterologist asked me if I was still driving, and when I said I was, he suggested I stop. He explained that another symptom of primary biliary cholangitis is confusion, and the medical term is hepatic encephalopathy. *HE is a condition that causes temporary worsening of brain function in people with advanced liver disease. When your liver is damaged it can no longer remove toxic substances from your blood. These toxins build up and can travel through your body until they reach your brain, causing mental and physical symptoms. HE often starts slowly, and at first you may not be aware you have it. The stages of HE span from mild to severe and symptoms vary depending on how bad your liver disease is.*[18]

I told the doctor I wasn't experiencing any confusion, and he said it could show up out of the blue without warning. Scary stuff. What happened in real life is that I thought I was losing my mind. It seemed like I was losing my independence and freedom when told I was no longer allowed to drive. While processing some of the emotions arising, I came up with a couple of questions to ask myself to look at my whole situation differently, *What new thoughts could I choose to be independent? What activities could I create to be empowered and free?* WOW—it amazed me how a couple of GOOD questions could shift my perspective. I learned the relationships that I nurture and

---

[17] https://www.iliveineasyworld.com/

[18] American Liver Foundation, Diagnosing Hepatic Encephalopathy

my positive thoughts empower me to develop connection, fulfillment, and pride. I believe life is a university that teaches me how to perceive things differently, create lasting relationships, and share my gifts with the world every day.

My doctor had a questionnaire for me to fill out that tracked the symptoms of hepatic encephalopathy—confusion. There were two categories, mental and physical. For the mental category, I had to be aware of any signs of forgetfulness, confusion, poor judgment, not knowing where I was or where I was going, and inappropriate behaviour. For the physical category, I had to be aware of changes in sleep patterns, worsening of handwriting, slurred speech, and slowed or sluggish movement.

Several days later, I was at work when the confusion showed up. I was performing a familiar task, and I couldn't remember how to do it, so I had to get help from a co-worker. The second incident occurred on December 24th during my lunch break. I was at a local mall that I had shopped at a million times, and when I proceeded to go back to work, I was confused and could not find the down escalator. It was a horrible feeling not knowing where I was since I had been in this place thousands of times before. Fortunately, I had been practising mindfulness, so I took deep breaths in and out and stayed calm, and the confusion passed.

Another incident was when I received a gift card from work and had placed it in my wallet. Then, one day, I decided to clean out my wallet and saw that card. I thought it was an old points card and cut it into tiny pieces. Several days later, I remembered the gift card, *Oh my gosh, where was it?* I panicked because I realized I'd cut it up. Then, I remembered it was in the garbage and retrieved it to tape it back together. There were several other incidences of confusion, and I thought I was

Chapter 7

losing my mind. It was really scary, and I could understand completely why the doctor suggested I not drive.

I was coping and accepted my symptoms well, but then, without any notice, I started having mood swings and became angry, sad, bitchy, and cranky. I also had negative thoughts about my husband being better off if I were dead. For the first time, I realized I needed to seek professional help and speak to a counsellor. One of the many benefits I received at work was having access to counsellors and professional help. I booked an appointment with a woman who listened with an open mind and heart. She assured me that my thoughts were normal and asked if I had shared my thoughts and fears with my husband. When I said I hadn't, she suggested it might be a good first step because we needed to be on the same page if we were going to get through the next few years. So, I had a conversation with my husband, and this knowledge reminded me that no man is an island, and I cannot do it alone. It? Life. Sometimes, I need help from my partner, friends, family, and, yes, even a professional. Also, I recognized that if I don't communicate what I am thinking and feeling with my partner, we can't possibly be on the same page.

There were far too many appointments to mention to prepare for my transplant surgery in Vancouver. However, the one that stands out above the rest was my root canal scheduled on December 14th, which happened to be my 60th birthday. It certainly wasn't on my list of how I wanted to celebrate, but it helped me realize I needed to celebrate my birthday that year. I had so much fun planning a girlfriends' lunch, sending out invitations, and creating a fridge magnet for each of my friends. The magnet read *I can live without fame and fortune—to live without friendship would be torture.*

My daughter drove down from Nanaimo, and I was honoured to celebrate with twenty wonderful friends.

Along with the confusion, I was retaining fluid. When a liver is in serious trouble, the body retains fluid in the legs, ankles, and feet. This occurs because impaired liver function inhibits the body's ability to produce and circulate proteins, which in turn causes circulatory issues. It was funny when someone asked me when my baby was due because I looked like I was eight months pregnant. Between my confusion and my big belly, I knew the day to leave work was drawing near. I felt terrible because I made a mistake on a client's pension. In late January, my team leader came to me with an application that I had processed incorrectly due to my confusion. I had a lot of pride in my work, and the last thing I wanted was to make mistakes processing client transactions. I lost confidence in my ability to do my job, and I seemed to have lost the knowledge and training I had learned. I knew it was time to take action to get the necessary paperwork in place to go on medical leave.

A few weeks prior to my decision, I received a phone call from my sister and brother-in-law, who were looking out for my health. They could deliver tough love, and because of my sister-in-law's medical background, she explained the importance of having some reserves in order to provide the best chance of a speedy and healthy recovery. Their tough love was instrumental in helping me recognize that leaving work was the best decision I could make to prepare for surgery. Since I wasn't on the transplant list and didn't know when I might be called, I didn't want to leave work too early. I was aware there is a two-year window between going through the entire transplant process and the possibility of returning to work. Since I didn't know my transplant date or how long my recovery could take, I didn't want to be off work too long before the actual surgery.

Chapter 7

I decided to follow my sister and brother-in-law's advice and take the necessary steps to prepare for medical leave. So, I made an appointment the same week with my doctor, and I went to get blood work done on my last day of work on February 5, 2016. I was only on medical leave for about a week when more fluid accumulated, and my abdominal girth began to increase. At 160 pounds, it was getting harder to walk, and I was coughing a lot due to the pressure on my diaphragm from the fluid build-up in my abdomen. Due to the increased pressure on my diaphragm, I experienced shortness of breath because the fluid also migrated across the diaphragm around my lungs. Since my liver was failing and fluid continued to build up, I required a therapeutic paracentesis procedure. A needle was carefully placed into the abdominal area, with a bag attached to it, and large amounts of fluid were slowly drained out. On any given appointment, up to five litres of fluid were removed.

For several months, I found myself at the hospital every two weeks receiving this treatment. It usually took four to six hours, but it was such a relief to lose some weight and breathe freely. My sister and brother-in-law came to visit in April, and I was in the poorest health I had ever been. I had an appointment the day after they arrived, and for some reason, only half of the normal amount of liquid was drained. The nurse told me if things got unbearable, I could go to emergency and have another paracentesis. When I returned home, I told them I was so disappointed that the procedure did not go well, and I wasn't much lighter.

I was back to 160 pounds only four days later, and once again, I could hardly walk or breathe. So, my husband took me to the emergency department in the wee hours of the morning. Since it was the weekend, the hospital staff needed to call a doctor in to perform the procedure as an emergency. This time it took eight hours. However, they drained nine litres of fluid and I was much lighter and able to breathe and move around freely for at least another week.

On April 28th, we were visiting with our sister and brother-in-law in our living room when we received the phone call that I was activated to the liver transplant waitlist. I know there are times in people's lives when they are elated to get the call, telling them they made the team, they were chosen to play a part in a play, or they got the job. However, there was no feeling like being told that the first part of my wait was over, and I made it on the transplant list. The criterion to be added to the waitlist is based on how sick you are, which is then measured on your Model for End-Stage Liver Disease—MELD—score. I was able to breathe a huge sigh of relief.

Chapter 7

My Recipe for Navigating Life With Symptoms

- *Self-care first—When I say yes to someone, am I saying no to myself?*
- *I am enough, I do enough, I have enough;*
- *Be present—Be here now*
- *Be Vulnerable—The ability to freely express my thoughts, feelings, desires, and opinions regardless of what others may think of me, even my boss and co-workers;*
- *Celebrate me and my birthday;*
- *Create ten mantras for health—A vision*

My Self-Reflection

Navigating life with symptoms was much easier once I learned to take care of myself first and let go of old beliefs and patterns that I wasn't good enough. Once I started to make mature decisions, face my fears by taking one small action step, and be vulnerable, life started to become more of an adventure than a struggle. I learned to celebrate my accomplishments and my birthday even when I was experiencing symptoms. I created a vision for my health and focused on my ten mantras instead of my current situation. I learned to be here now and cherish the moments I have with others.

Evolving To Be Me

What is Your Recipe For Navigating Life With Symptoms?

Chapter 7

Given Your Recipe, Share Your Self-Reflection

VIII

I Kissed Death, But Wouldn't Let It Hug Me

*I will not die without fighting for
a life I am not yet done living.*

~ Bethany Wiggins

Could I pass the final test? About three weeks before being activated to the transplant list, my gastroenterologist called to inquire why I had not been placed yet. I indicated that I thought it was because the cardiac angiogram had not been done yet. He said he was going to call the transplant coordinator to expedite its scheduling. I could be activated to the list if my heart was healthy enough to sustain a major operation—the final test. My doctor was concerned about my size, and fluid retention putting pressure on my diaphragm, which made it difficult to breathe and walk.

The finer details of the angiogram are boring. However, I was given a local anesthetic to numb my upper leg, and the hardest part of the whole procedure was getting myself from the gurney to the operating table and back while keeping my leg straight. My husband was in the waiting room, losing his mind because they told him the procedure might only take a couple of hours unless there were complications. I was the last patient in the recovery room, so he had vivid thoughts about what could be taking so long. Nevertheless, I think this medical appointment prepared him in some small way for what was looming around the corner.

I left the hospital around six that evening and had very little to eat. I needed to keep my leg straight and received instructions to stay overnight in a hotel. My discharge instructions included not bending or squatting, not lifting anything over ten pounds for three days, keeping my leg straight for 48 hours, and not using stairs. I booked a different hotel from the first one because it had stairs, so I was exhausted by the time I checked in and ordered take-out. Of all the procedures I had going back and forth to Vancouver over a three-year period, that one was the most challenging due to my size and exhaustion.

Asking for help was not something my husband and I were good at. Since we had known about me needing a liver transplant for years, we believed we should have been the ones planning for it financially, emotionally, and logistically. At one of our pre-transplant appointments, the social worker asked what family members could be advocates for me while in the hospital and when I transitioned to my home away from home in Vancouver. During our decision-making process, my husband and I never thought to ask any of our family for help; we assumed it was our problem to solve, and we could handle it.

The sister and brother-in-law who helped me decide to leave work also helped my husband and me with literature and tough love, and they also asked pertinent questions months before I received the call. In addition, they helped us plan better by indicating the need for advocates for the hospital stay, as well as support after being released from the hospital. Obviously,

Chapter 8

without the support of family and friends who volunteered to help, I may not have had the same positive outcome.

One of the forms I received was titled *Social Support for Transplantation*. This form was filled out by people who agreed to support me during my hospital stay and while living in Vancouver post-transplant. Asking people to travel across the country and spend their time and money was another step towards being vulnerable. I made a list of friends who I wanted to support me, knowing that some of them might not be able to. I told them they were on my list, and I wanted their support but knew that timing wasn't right for them.

Once I was activated to the liver transplant waitlist, I knew it was time to take some action towards creating a financial plan. After having a conversation with my sister, who came to visit several weeks later, I took another step towards being vulnerable and started a Go Fund Me. This was a way to enable family, friends, and colleagues to support me financially through my journey. It took a lot of courage to write up my story and reach out to others for help. I learned that people want to support those they care about, and the Go Fund Me gave them that opportunity.

My husband and I were grocery shopping a few weeks after my trip to the emergency department to have the fluid drained, and I received a call from my gastroenterologist. He told me that my sodium was dangerously low and advised me to keep my paracentesis appointment—draining fluid from my abdomen—which was scheduled for the next day. Once the procedure was finished, he arranged to have me transported by ambulance to the hospital he worked out of. The procedure went well, and I was whisked off to the other hospital by ambulance around supper time. No lights were flashing, and no sirens were blasting, but it was my first ride in the back of an ambulance. The paramedics were very skilled and had some entertaining stories to tell along the way.

Once I arrived at the hospital, I was given intravenous fluids and electrolyte replacement every few hours. My daily liquid intake was reduced to manage the concentration of sodium in my blood. I was kept in over the weekend until my sodium levels were managed. My daughter, son-in-law, and grandson came to visit along with a few friends, and the hospital food was extremely good. I was discharged and returned home on a Monday, June 13, 2016.

There are two life situations when I'm ecstatic to get a midnight phone call. One is when someone near and dear to my heart has a baby, and the other occurred when I was told that years of escalating symptoms and waiting were over—they found a lifesaving liver. This was a happy day for me, but in my heart, I knew it was a sad day for someone else because they had lost a loved one. I am forever grateful for the one simple action that person took to sign their organ donor card. That one signature saved my life, and I hope others will consider making that decision as well. It was nine in the morning on June 14, 2016, I was 60 years old, and they told me to be on the next ferry.

It seemed like a miracle that I could receive a liver within six weeks of getting on the transplant list. I got a good picture of how I lived my day-to-day life that morning. There was a weekend's worth of dishes all over the counter and piles of paper strewn all over my desk. It's amazing how fast two people can get organized and get stuff done when someone lights a fire under their collective butts, so to speak. It must have looked like a three-ring circus while both my husband and I ran around our house like chickens with our heads cut off. I had read lots of material about preparation for the call, so

Chapter 8

I did have a file of important documents at my fingertips which helped relieve some anxiousness.

My husband was running his own business and needed to call some of his clients, send emails, and tidy up some loose ends. It was interesting packing for a journey, not knowing my return date, and I wondered what life might look like when I returned. Although anytime I take a vacation, go on a trip, or visit family, I am not always certain how life will look when I return.

We spent our ferry trip contacting relatives and business associates about our up-and-coming adventure. I realize not everyone perceives checking into a hospital for a major operation as an adventure, but I did. We dropped our dog off at our son's place in Vancouver and checked in at the emergency department desk since the transplant clinic was closed. While I waited to be admitted, I made a telephone call to the coordinator of an apartment that was earmarked specifically for liver transplant patients. I had contacted Karen Stacey several times before. She created the *Happy Liver Society* and opened Stacey House—a home-away-from-home for liver transplant patients. The nurse arrived to take me to my room at the same time, so I told her I had to call her back later.

My husband had no idea where he might spend the night or stay for the next few days, so while I waited to get prepped for surgery, I called Karen back. She told me the previous occupants had just moved out of Stacey House and arranged a time for my husband to pick up the keys that night. Only 17 hours had passed from when I got the call, packed my bag, rode the ferry, dropped off our dog, and was prepped for surgery to when my husband had a place to live. It seemed like I was watching the next phase of life unfold in slow motion.

A few weeks after I left work on medical leave, I got a

call from SunLife Insurance, who was handling my disability claim. The adjuster proceeded to ask me questions about my day-to-day life. He wanted to know if I was still friends with the people I worked with and if I thought I'd be returning to work. At first, I was really annoyed because, in my mind, my application clearly stated I was on a waitlist for a liver transplant. *Sheesh,* I thought, *how do I know? I haven't even had the transplant yet!* When I was a public servant, I always did my best to empathize with the pensioner. However, following policies and legislation was part of my job. Therefore, I reminded myself I was performing my duties to the best of my ability. This thought helped me with my liver transplant journey and still does to this day. Anytime I stand in front of someone serving me, or I'm on the phone talking to someone or on a chat on my computer, I remind myself the person I am interacting with is doing their job. I choose to believe they are like me and doing the best they can.

Two of the best nurses in the transplant wing of the hospital greeted me with open arms. I immediately decided that all medical staff were doing their jobs, and they knew how to do them. My role was to trust them and the process. I had my first liver transplant on June 15, 2016, and the surgeon called my husband to tell him that it took a little over five hours and went extremely well. The first thing I remember after waking up in the ICU is my son standing at my bedside. I was overwhelmed with emotion and unable to speak because I had a breathing tube. I motioned for a piece of paper and pen but was too weak to write anything down. It wasn't a very private place, with four patients in each room.

I was in a lot of pain and had so many IVs that I looked like a pincushion. Two nurses were helping each other put in an IV, and it really hurt. I found relief when I looked at the

Chapter 8

nurse's arm covered in a tattoo of a gumball machine; it made me smile. The nursing staff in the ICU was truly amazing, and each patient had one nurse to look after them. The breathing tube came out a day or two after the operation, and I got to have liquids. The physiotherapists had me up and sitting in a chair, and I could walk around the ward within a few days of the surgery. Most patients leave the ICU in their bed, but the medical team believed I was strong enough to return to the transplant ward by wheelchair. My sister-in-law from Toronto was my first advocate to arrive a few days after the transplant. She and I got settled into the room quite nicely, and then my temperature spiked, and I threw up; I had to bid farewell to my transplant room and was sent back to the ICU.

Although the transplant went well, my spleen was enlarged and created complications for my new liver. Several weeks after my transplant, my sister and brother-in-law arrived from Calgary. I was scheduled for a coil embolization of the splenic artery—an operation to block the blood flow to the artery to the spleen. The operation was scheduled on three different occasions, and fasting the night before was part of the process, which means no food until after the operation. I was not notified that my surgery was cancelled until after the kitchen was closed, and in my case, I had very little to eat for several days in a row and was famished. My sister and brother-in-law advocated for me and saved the day by bringing me some fried rice. It was the best fried rice I had ever eaten.

All I remember about the procedure was that I was the last one operated on that day, I had to lie flat on my back, not move, and it was painful. One of the technicians was getting married in a few months, and she was talking about her wedding plans. Another one spoke about herself. I remember that the radio was on because it took my mind off what was happening to me. The whole process took several hours, and I was exhausted the next day. Many visitors came to see me that day—my niece from Edmonton, my daughter from Nanaimo, my son and his family from Vancouver, and my sister and brother-in-law from Calgary, who were still with me as my advocates.

Due to my enlarged spleen throwing off blood clots that accumulated around my liver, causing it to fail, they performed an operation to shrink the spleen enough to stop it from throwing off more clots. The operation did not go as planned, so I was scheduled for surgery to remove the blood clots around my liver a few days later. I remember going down to surgery with the perception it was just another procedure, all part of the process. I regained consciousness five days later.

As I lay in a drug-induced state, I was oblivious to the anguish my husband and family were going through. This part of the journey is written from my husband's perspective. He was in Victoria the night the doctors cleaned out the blood clots. Once they opened me up, they realized they were too late. It was 11:30 at night on July 8, 2016, the worst day of my husband's life because he got an urgent phone call from the doctor, telling him to get to the hospital as fast as possible. This is not a call anyone wants to get, and I don't imagine any doctor wants to make it. He was already on the ferry and arrived at the hospital an hour later.

Someone was with me the entire time, and when my husband arrived, my sister and brother-in-law were by my bedside. His sister told him she knew something was wrong because they returned me to my room too soon. My husband says he will be forever grateful to all the family members who helped him get through this devastating ordeal. When he got to the hospital, the attending doctor called him into a private room and my husband told him that his sister needed to be with him because he didn't think he could go in alone. He could tell that the doctor wasn't happy when he described the procedures they had performed and told him that the liver was already dying—there was nothing more that could be done. He said they brought me back to the ICU, and the doctor suggested he call everyone because he thought I might not make it through the night.

He told the doctor, *Well, I'm pretty much fucked because she is my world, so please don't let that happen.* My family sat on pins and needles as they collectively held their breath and prayed for a miracle. My husband tells me the best day of his life was Sunday morning, July 10th, when the surgical team showed up in the room. However, at first, he thought it was to say good-bye to me. The head surgeon calmed my husband's fears and told him they were taking me away because they had found another liver that was being flown in from one of the eastern provinces. The doctor said he would call my husband when the operation was done. My husband recalls this being the happiest day of his life and showed me the video he took of them taking me to the operating room for the second transplant. As he sat beside my bed that day and a half, he heard a line in a song, *The Dance* by Garth Brooks, play over and over in his mind—*I could have missed the pain, but I'd have had to miss the dance.*

When I gained full consciousness, I was oblivious to any of this and remembered things as they had been, not as they currently were. Over the next few months, my husband and other family members proceeded to fill me in on what I'd missed. My sister, daughter, son, and their spouses provided a calming effect on my husband, who never left my side during those few days I fought for my life. My entire family rallied together to pray while the transplant team searched country-wide for another lifesaving liver.

What I do remember about those five days were the hallucinations and dreams I had due to the medications I was given. They were so vivid that I remember them to this day. Some may call one of my hallucinations a near-death encounter, or as I like to describe it, *I kissed death, but I wouldn't let it hug me.* I was on a gurney, and someone pushed me down a hallway. I remember saying, *Take me to the angels; I need to see the angels.* I sensed I was racing against a clock, against time, and the person pushing me wasn't going fast enough. I could see a bright light at the end of the hall, and my heart was racing. Internally, I was in panic mode. I reached a point in this journey down the hall where I realized there was no turning back if I went any further. Every part of me wanted to live and stay here in this realm on Earth. I knew in my heart that it wasn't my time. It was time to fight because I wasn't done living yet.

Once I realized there was no turning back, I urgently screamed, *no, no, no, not those angels, the Earth angels, the Earth angels, turn around, turn around,* and gratefully the person pushing the gurney immediately turned it around. I knew this was not where I was meant to go and noticed a great sense of relief, and I knew in my heart of hearts I had turned a corner. I was already with the Earth angels, and I was staying here on Earth with them. I remember hearing my mother's voice's saying, *It's going to be Okay. God has you in his arms; remember you are God's child, and he loves you.* I thought of my young grandbabies and knew I wasn't ready to leave them just yet. They were meant to know who I was, and I was meant to hear the precious word *grandma* fall from their lips. I also had a grandson I was getting to know, and I was looking forward to having him come and stay at grandma's house for many years to come.

On July 11, 2016, while I teetered between life and death,

they located a second liver, and another life-giving operation was performed. Did I have a near-death encounter? I don't know. But I do know I wasn't ready to die, and kissing death was close enough for me. Some events or dates are unforgettable. But that day—the day I received a second chance at life—fills my heart and soul with gratitude and awe, and it will remain as a truly magical and defining moment like no other.

It was only 100 days from the day I was admitted to the hospital to the day I was discharged, and this was day 27. My sister-in-law from Toronto is an expert in risk management, and she created a binder she brought with her on her first visit. The binder was titled *The Caregiver's Guide* and had helping hands on the cover. Each of my advocates signed their names on the hands; it served as a reference book and included a list of caregiver responsibilities. The three basics to follow were: be attentive to signs of deterioration, error on the side of caution by alerting the healthcare team, and do not talk yourself out of being worried. In addition, there was a section for my caregivers to write down my blood pressure, temperature, pain level from zero to ten, nausea, heart rate, and emotions. She also included a list of personal care items like socks with grips for walking and warmth, a pillow for legs while sleeping, and a special shawl for comfort.

The binder included literature entitled *The Empowered Patient* and *Ten Things Patients Should Know*. It also had excellent information from a Toronto liver transplant manual that included topics on monitoring for rejection and infection, complications encountered in the early post-transplant period, possible long-term complications, and what the patient, caregivers, and supporters can be aware of and expect. This binder helped me and my caregivers support me to climb back up the mountain to health. She also ensured I had a notebook to write down questions for the medical staff, along with their answers. As a result, my advocates and I could understand what was going on with my body on a day-to-day basis. My sister-in-law named my new liver Oliver, which is a play on words O-liver, and I thought it was the perfect name.

Once I gained some strength and returned to the transplant ward, I learned some medical terminology and what the nurses looked for when they took my blood pressure, temperature, and heart rate. They measured my abdominal girth, asked questions about pain in my belly, nausea, glucose levels, respiratory rate, headaches, etcetera. During our pre-transplant meetings, I was informed there may be mood swings and personality and emotional changes after the transplant. I learned how important it was to understand the results of my blood work and what certain medical terms meant. When I didn't understand something, I wrote down questions, and the doctors or nurses were more than happy to answer. They know an engaged and aware patient will heal quicker and can leave the hospital sooner.

My biggest challenge was eating hospital food. My daughter and son-in-law gave me a journal for visitors to write in, which helped me when I presumed I was all alone. One of my friends wrote *suck it up, buttercup*. However, there were times when it was extremely hard to eat the food without throwing up. One of the issues was that I am celiac, and there were not many gluten-free choices. My one sister-in-law suggested I say an affirmation to myself over and over while eating, *Food is medicine, food is medicine*. My other sister-in-law sent me an email full of movie quotes such as *Do or do not, there is no try* by Yoda, *Are you crying – there is no crying in baseball* from the movie A League of Their Own, *I'm as mad as hell, and I'm not going to take this anymore* by Howard Beale from the movie

Chapter 8

Network. A few quotes I resonated with were *This too shall pass* by Abraham Lincoln and *Inch by inch, life's a cinch. Yard by yard, life's hard* by John Bytheway.

Music was a huge comfort during my entire hospital stay, and I listened to motivating songs, such as *We are the Champions* by Queen, *Amazing Grace* by John Newton, *Don't stop Believin'* by Journey, and *Trust in You* by Lauren Daigle. There were too many to list, but all this advice and action helped tremendously.

At first, my caregivers helped me track the food I ate because gaining weight was another measure for being well enough to leave the hospital. They also helped me prepare my medication for the day, and at one point, I was taking 25 different prescriptions. I needed to eat between 1500 to 2000 calories, and since my fluid intake was restricted to 1.5 litres, the calories could not include beverages. This was because my sodium level was extremely low, and it was challenging because I disliked hospital food. To this day, my calorie intake includes beverages. Increasing my sodium level was one of the criteria needed to be well enough to be discharged, and it was also a challenging problem for the doctors to solve.

The ICU nurse asked three questions every day, *Who are you, where are you, and what is the date?* I always knew my name and where I was, but there was a period in the ICU when I struggled with the date. In fact, sometimes, I thought it was the month of June when it was July. I interpret these three questions differently today. Who are you? A wife, a mother, a writer, a woman, a retiree, a granmudder, and a spiritual being having a human experience. When my children were young, they called me mudder, therefore, it seemed fitting once I had grandchildren to refer to myself as granmudder. Am I a poet, a writer, a musician, a healer, or an observer? Yes, maybe some of the above. Where am I? I'm at home, in British Columbia,

Canada, on planet Earth. What is the date? I have a calendar on my wall, so I'm always aware of the date. I've realized these are three excellent questions to ask myself every day from a philosophical versus healing and recovery perspective.

When I was in the ICU and *out of it*, the doctor and nursing staff were on top of managing my pain. Pain control was not something I really thought about before surgery. It was up to me to let the nurse know when I was in pain by giving her a score from one to ten. The hospital rule was that pain meds could usually be administered every four hours. I distinctly recall rationalizing with myself one night because I didn't want to become addicted to pains meds— I believed I could tough it out and go longer than four hours. When the night nurse checked on me, she asked what my pain level was on a scale of one to ten, and I told her it was eight. So, she asked me why I didn't ask for pain meds. I told her my rationale, and she told me that was ridiculous, explaining that pain management is part of the healing process and good pain control can prevent pneumonia and blood clots. I was grateful for her knowledge and that she showed up when she did. *You're not going to be in pain on my watch*, she said to me more than once.

I vividly recall one incident when I was in a lot of pain and hadn't slept well. I was lying in bed early one morning when several doctors came in. One part of their morning routine was to poke and prod my belly. One of the doctors, who I did not recognize, pushed on my stomach very hard, and I thought I'd pass out from the pain. Another doctor entered the room about an hour later, and I assertively said, *Don't touch me*. He threw his hands in the air and said, I won't. My sister-in-law from Calgary was with me, and after he left, she told me that he wasn't the same doctor who had pushed on my stomach earlier. We had a good laugh over that. Or rather, I chuckled—it hurt too much to laugh.

The first type of exercises they asked me to do were those I could do on the bed for my toes, legs, arms, and hands. I remember not liking the bed exercises very much, but they were designed to strengthen my core. I realized if I wanted to gain strength, I needed to make them part of my daily routine. Several weeks later, a young full-of-life physiotherapist bounced into my room in the ICU and suggested I get up and sit in a chair. I thought, *Are you kidding me? Go away, I am not getting up, let alone sitting in a chair?* She didn't listen, and she was not going away. She won and helped me get into the chair. I was not worried, believing I could handle sitting there for about 30 minutes. However, two hours later, she finally returned to a very unhappy person—ME! It was a bit challenging getting back into bed, and I decided I didn't like her one little bit. I figured it was no big deal because I didn't have to work with her again once I was moved to the transplant ward.

You can imagine my enthusiasm when I found out she was also the physiotherapist for the transplant ward! She bounced in at different times each day to ensure I got up, sat in a chair, and did my bed exercises. One day, I didn't want to get out of bed for physio, so I didn't. As a result, it was even harder to get up the next day, and I learned it's the step-by-step, day-to-day action that creates a habit and, in this case, builds strength and muscle. In every situation, others can influence me in positive or negative ways. I realized my physiotherapist was my new best friend and the person who could help me get stronger and eventually get out of the hospital. She left Vancouver General Hospital just before I was released, and I was assigned another physiotherapist. I missed her because I realized I needed her to challenge me to work hard to achieve my goal of getting stronger every day.

A doctor came in to see me in early August and indicated that part of the recovery program was going to rehabilitation. As a result, I could expect to be in the hospital for at least five more weeks. I took this on as a challenge, deciding I would do whatever was required not to go to rehabilitation. With the help of my physiotherapist, I worked hard every day at doing my bed exercises and sitting in my wheelchair for most meals. I eventually got strong enough to get up to go to the bathroom, and I used my IV pole for balance and to walk around my room. I repeated my affirmations as I walked one foot in front of the other, *Inch by inch, life's a cinch*. After several weeks, I was strong enough to walk around the hospital ward with my IV pole. Eventually, I could walk to the kitchen and back and even visit the outdoor terrace to enjoy the fresh air and sunshine in the courtyard. I was in the hospital for eight more weeks due to some medical issues that were out of my control that the doctors needed to sort out. I did not have to go to rehabilitation because getting physically stronger was in my power, and I learned to focus on what I could control instead of what I could not.

I discovered that it is not what happens in life but rather the meaning I place on it that causes me suffering. When I was in the ICU, I had many medical tests, and I never placed a bad or a good meaning on any of them. Sometimes, I heard medical terms that scared me, like rejection or embolization, and I could have worried or thought negatively about them. However, when a doctor shared a medical description with me, I took it as a fact, part of the process, a reality; *it is what it is*. My perception is that nothing is ever good or bad. However, the meaning I place on it is what makes it good or bad.

Chapter 8

I also learned that when I argue with my reality, I lose 100 percent of the time. There were many times when I had an agenda and made plans that I wanted to stick to come hell or high water. However, in the hospital, arguing with reality was a losing game. So, I decided to enjoy the process, connect with the nurses, learn everyone's name, be in the moment, take one day at a time, and be grateful for each day. I continue to carry this lesson with me, knowing that I lose when I argue with reality.

For me, the most important quality I needed in the hospital was patience. I often say, *Patients need patience too*. Joyce Myers says, *Patience is not simply the ability to wait—it's how we behave while we're waiting*. Everything happens in due time, and my situation won't stay this way forever. It is a balance of looking to the future, thinking things will get better, believing I will get better, being in the present, and knowing that I can handle each day with grace, love, and kindness.

It's very easy to lose perspective in times of illness, but it was important for me to have hope and see my life unfold positively. But I realized there is always someone dealing with a more critical situation. I also know that whatever situation I find myself in, I MUST focus on a positive outcome. At that moment, no matter how big or small, I must take whatever action I can—even if it's eating a spoonful of peanut butter or doing my bed exercises. They were baby steps towards healing, recovery, and having a healthy body and positive future.

There were some challenging situations when I needed patience, humour, and compassion for others. It wasn't all about me. Little did I know that when you're in the hospital in the transplant ward, you can get shipped out of your room. Not for bad behavior, but to make room for those who are in poorer health than you. Since I was in the hospital for 100

Evolving To Be Me

days, I got shipped out several times, but it was only down the hall to a different unit and a different nursing staff. One time, I was moved to a ward used for patients who were only in the hospital for three to four days. Most of them had a minor issue to deal with, such as having a kidney stone removed, and they could recover at home.

I had a lot of personal items, and my husband had his own chair since he was there often.

The room was made to accommodate four patients with individual spots with curtains for privacy. It became very crowded when they added me and my bed in the middle of the room with no curtains, plugins, or outlets for oxygen, etcetera. The bathroom was shared, and the room was co-ed. It was quite the contrast from having a private room, and I certainly needed patience and a sense of humour in this situation. The nurses were mortified, and I was sure one extraordinarily kind and compassionate nurse wanted to cry. Some of the nursing staff took up their concerns with the head nurse. However, they said nothing could be done. They strung an extension cord from one of the other cubicles to my area, so I could plug in the bed to adjust it up or down. Anyone who visited the patients in the two cubicles in the corner had to walk right through my space. I think I was there for about three days when a lady visiting her husband took the time to come over to me and said, *This must be challenging for you, but you will get through it one breath at a time.* I was grateful for her kindness because I was seen by a total stranger. I recognize the value of seeing and hearing people in day-to-day interactions with them.

One night, I had to go to the bathroom and wasn't walking very well. I had to drag my IV pole with me, extension cord, and all. I stumbled just before I got to the door, and several nurses came running. The nurse assigned to me stood outside of the bathroom until I was done, and on my way back to the non-cubicle, we both started laughing. It seemed so comical, me in my hospital gown, dragging my IV pole across the room in the middle of the night. I got through it one breath at a time and was moved back to a private room and remained there until I was discharged.

I think about the Academy Awards when someone wins an Oscar. Everyone says thanks to those who helped them along the way. I wish there was a forum to thank the doctors, nurses, and medical staff at Vancouver General Hospital. I might not be writing this today without the support and kindness I received from my advocates, family, friends, and strangers. Music also helped me during my 100 days in the hospital. There were several weeks after the second transplant when I was in a lot of pain and not well enough to have my iPhone. There was a radio in my room, and my husband found an oldies station. While in pain, I listened to Petula Clark, the Beach Boys, Tommy James, and the Shondells. That radio station and those songs led me through some dark nights towards solace.

As I got stronger, I listened to many songs on my iPhone, too many to list here, but there were a few that I sang hundreds of times. *Don't Stop Believing* by Journey became a great song to live my life by. No matter what is going on in and around me, I believe my situation will get better, and my life will improve—this too shall pass. When I sing or say the words to this song, I think of believing in humanity, in myself, in a higher power, and that I am surrounded by people who believe in me. My husband recorded a playlist entitled *Sleepy Time* that had a lot of Lord of the Rings tunes and songs by Enya, which were very relaxing and helped me sleep. I think music is something most people love because it supports them to experience joy, love, and peace. It can provide connection in a way that inspires them to be themselves and freely express who they are as individuals while sharing something they love with others. Music can be a true healer for the heart, mind, and soul.

Another song that helped me was *Long as I Can See the Light* by Creedence Clearwater Revival. I knew that literally being able to see the light at the end of the tunnel had a significant impact on my healing process. I visualized myself being discharged from the hospital and living at Stacey House. I was grateful the transplant team knew patients needed a home away from home after they were discharged because I certainly wasn't ready to go straight home. I could see myself getting stronger and stronger and then walking over to Stacey House, which did take several attempts and several weeks, but I did it. I visualized myself spending time there with family and friends.

Chapter 8

My Recipe For Kissing Death But Not Letting It Hug Me

- *Fight to live, I only have one life; and no one was coming for my liver;*
- *Look at where I am going, not where I was;*
- *Patients need patience too;*
- *Take action; it doesn't matter how small;*
- *Trust my support network; they have my best interest in mind;*
- *Set daily goals and create habits; it's part of the recovery process.*

My Self-Reflection

Looking back on this part of my journey, I can say scars are tattoos with better stories. I learned valuable lessons prior to my surgeries that helped me through two liver transplants. I recognized life is a journey, not a destination. The past does not equal the future, whatever happens in life is happening for me not to me, and it is how I respond, not react, in any given situation that makes the difference. What I do with this one precious life I have been given is up to me, and I can always change my thoughts, behaviours, and beliefs. I can determine what success looks like and what is most important. I can connect my dots looking backwards and acknowledge all the lessons I learned and the people who supported me. My resilience, and being driven, saved me in more ways than one.

What is Your Recipe For Kissing Death But Not Letting It Hug You?

Chapter 8

Given Your Recipe, Share Your Self-Reflection

IX

Recovery is a Team Effort

My brother-in-law in Toronto oversaw making a list of people who could support me either in the hospital or Stacey House and for how long and when. The schedule could be adjusted since I didn't know my discharge date. My sister-in-law was my first advocate and flew in from Toronto right after my first surgery and flew back with her husband and son after my second transplant. Her knowledge, compassion, and friendship made an enormous difference the first few weeks after my second transplant. My son and my daughter-in-law, who live in Vancouver, took over after they left and spent that summer by my side four days a week and tag-teamed their role. They juggled their schedules, along with my grandchildren, a seven-year-old and an eight-month-old baby. I was reminded of *I get by with a little help from my friends* by John Lennon.

There are so many events, gifts, involvements, and people who were part of my journey to recovery. Many family members were with me every step of the way, either in person or in thought and prayer. No words can describe the outpouring of love, care, and compassion I sensed from so many during my weakest days. Having their love and support got me through all my trials and tribulations during my transplant surgery and beyond.

I acknowledge that my process was not only about me but also about the people who sat by my bedside. They took their vacation, flew across the country, drove miles, took ferries, and purchased food and supplies. Family members prayed at home while wanting to be with me. And there were hundreds of people who prayed for me when I went through my dark night of the soul. I believe they may have had their own fears—demons to confront and obstacles that needed to be overcome.

I know the patient's journey is different than that of the people in their life. I can only imagine what it must have been like for my family members and advocates, seeing me hooked up to every single machine one could imagine. I know it was equally difficult for those praying from afar, not knowing whether I might live or die.

My daughter and her husband were at my bedside when they could be, and even when I was drugged up, I sensed their presence. I've learned that I have more senses than the five I learned about growing up. I always had a loved one on the other end of the phone when I needed my spirits lifted. My mom was a comfort to me on a few low days because she was always home, and she was a good listener; I knew how much she loved and cared for me. My father-in-law always provided comfort by letting me know many people were praying for me. Thanks to all the supporters I had in the hospital, I have a daily written journal of who visited, what tests I had done, how I was feeling, what doctors came in, and all the questions and concerns they addressed.

Friendships have always been extremely important to me, and I don't believe I can have too many meaningful relationships. Many of the nurses became my friends even though it was temporary. I knew how important it was to remember their first names and became famous as the *patient who remembered*.

Chapter 9

I think it brought a smile to their faces, and they looked forward to caring for me. Now that I am out of the hospital, I cherish my memories of these amazing heroes and think of them often. Each one did their part to help me heal and get well enough to leave the hospital. They have compassion for all their patients and envision them as being well. They see each one of us walking out of the hospital and then returning for a visit as vibrantly healthy individuals, even when the patients often can't see this themselves.

Ten Best things for Receiving Oliver—Each holds the same importance:

1. The Vancouver General Hospital doctors, interns, and residents;
2. I loved seeing the VGH nurses' smiling faces and hearing their stories;
3. All hospital staff because they helped through my healing process;
4. Warm blankets—a hospital secret; there was nothing better than a warm blanket;
5. Visitors—friends or family; there is nothing better than feeling connected and loved;
6. Flowers, cards, and gifts—flowers brightened my room. A few treasured gifts: handmade shawl from my sister-in-law, a cute teddy bear dressed in a pink robe with *get well soon* embroidered on the collar from a friend, and a tree of life necklace I purchased to meditate on how precious life is and help me picture growth and a positive, healthy future;
7. My iPhone, music, phone calls, text messages, connection through social media, family pictures and cards that were posted where I could see them;

8. Food brought in from outside of the hospital—my advocates made sure I had snacks, and my son and daughter-in-law brought in homemade dinners. My husband scouted every store in Vancouver to find gluten-free food that I could prepare myself. These store-bought items are not something I eat these days. *Hell No*. With a military background, my husband said, *Those are field rations*;
9. Trips out of the room—exploring the gift shop, the coffee shop, and the cafeteria.
10. Day Passes—when I was well enough, my husband and I went to Stacey House to eat a gluten-free macaroni and cheese he had made. For the second day pass, we went out for ribs.

Through my interactions with others, I learned that part of my recovery process was not only healing my physical body. I found my faith was tested, and my spiritual health needed tending to. I found turning off the outside world helped me connect to others. I chose not to watch TV or listen to negative conversations by putting in headphones when possible. I learned that shifting my thoughts and attitudes was just as important for healing as medicine and healing is an act of faith for me. The word, ACT, looms as large as the faith it requires. The roles people played in my daily life became extremely important, and everyone's words of encouragement helped me take another step forward and gain strength.

I've always believed in karma and the familiar saying *what goes around comes around*. I believed this was true before my transplant, and I know it to be true today. I was blessed to be supported by friends, family, and hospital staff—even strangers—for many months. I believe asking others for help is a gift to both the giver and the receiver. It connects me to other human beings and helps me identify kindred spirits. I didn't always take care of my body and took it for granted. I smoked heavily for about twelve years but quit when I was pregnant with my daughter. I believe this was a gift I gave myself, and I may not have survived two liver transplants had I not quit. There were years when I was downright mean to my body and pushed myself mentally and physically to get *it* done. I recall not loving myself very much in my younger years, and I slapped my face or pulled my hair. I'm grateful for the lessons I received from doing the inner healing work to love and accept myself.

I thank my body every day for being a loyal servant, for getting me through the tough times, through ups and downs, and thick and thin. Even when I didn't treat it with love and kindness, it did everything to keep me alive during my two liver transplants. My body has fought like a lion, knowing I haven't finished my earth schooling. I am committed to taking care of my body by feeding it nourishing food and fluids and making sure I get enough rest and exercise. I treat it with loving-kindness and listen to what it needs.

I am grateful to have been supported by friends who were only a phone call away and travelled from Victoria to visit. One friend offered our family members a place to stay if Stacey House was full. A dear friend from work looked after our Cairn Terrier Jack Russell cross for over five months and then found him a good home. I trust any friend of mine, who I haven't written a story about in this memoir, knows that they played a huge part in my recovery.

When I asked my doctors why it took so long to recover from my second transplant, they reminded me that I had been hit by a Mack truck twice. So, it was no surprise to them that it could take much longer to recover after the second transplant. I often reflect on rule six of the *Rules for Being Human* by Cheri Carter Scott, which states, *There is no better than here. When your there has become a here, you will simply obtain another there that will, again, look better than here.*[19] I wanted to get out of the hospital, which was *here* in order to go to Stacey House which was *there*, but when I got to Stacey House, it became *here*, and I wanted to go home, which was now *there*. I remind myself of this rule every day, and it helps me be grateful for the moment, and I'm learning to be patient and happy where I am right now. Each day is a beautiful gift, and what I do with that gift is what really matters.

Once I gained my strength, I was curious why I wasn't being discharged from the hospital. The doctors were reluctant to give a date because they considered me a patient whose health could take a turn out of the blue, and I could end up dangling from a cliff. I decided to ask a seasoned nurse, and she obliged me by writing these three steps on my whiteboard:

1. Three consecutive blood tests, showing I no longer had an antibiotic-resistant bacterium;
2. The shunt that was put in during the transplant needed to be removed;
3. A drain was inserted on August 23rd to allow the fluid to drain from my spleen. Once the fluid was reduced, I could be discharged with it intact.

I learned that everything I was involved in has made me stronger. I understand that my point of power is in the present moment, and I can choose to be happy or angry; I can choose to be kind or mean; and I can choose to be a warrior or a whiner!

---

[19] https://www.drcherie.com/ten-rules-for-being-human

Chapter 9

I guess in the eyes of my family, I picked being a warrior. My sister-in-law gave me the name of Warrior Princess. I received a handmade bracelet with the word *Warrior* engraved in the leather from my husband's cousin from Fearless hART.[20]

Once I moved to Stacey House, I perceived a sense of freedom—freedom from routines, interruptions, other people's agendas, terrible food, and being woken up in the night. The day I was released was very exciting and also emotional because it was bittersweet, saying goodbye to everyone who played a role in saving me and giving me a second chance. Having this home away from home was the next phase of healing. I was weaker than I thought, and I still had a long way to complete recovery. I was so grateful to have someone stay with me for those eight and a half weeks.

My brother-in-law sent me a copy of the schedule, so I knew who was coming and for how long. My husband stayed for about ten days, and then my good friend from Nanaimo stayed for about a week. Anyone who came helped with household chores, cooking, transportation, shopping, laundry, bandage changes, healing, taking me to appointments and everything in between. My sister and brother-in-law returned from Calgary, and they pushed me in the wheelchair when we went on several outings and day trips. They ordered dinner in on several occasions and helped my husband cook a beautiful thanksgiving dinner enjoyed by the four of us and our son and his family. Stacey House donated all the fixings, and my sister-in-law ensured we had a gluten-free pie.

The day my sister and her husband left, they picked up my brother and sister-in-law from the airport. They had just flown in from Edmonton during a severe rain and windstorm.

---

[20] fearlesshart.ca

Fortunately, their flight was not delayed. We took the bus to Gastown and enjoyed lunch and a rainy day downtown. We had planned a trip to Granville Island, but I wasn't well enough to go, and I ended up back in the hospital due to low sodium levels for the last weekend they were visiting. So, they went to Granville Island on their own and brought me some gluten-free treats. I was released in time to accompany my husband while he drove them to the airport, and we saw them off.

We all enjoyed some movies, talked, laughed, and shared meals every day. It was a special time for me because I built stronger relationships with each of my family members and friends. It was very healing to reach out to any of them when I wanted to chat. It was the end of October, and my husband and I were chomping at the bit to return home to Victoria. The transplant team did not want to send me home too early, fearing I might have to return due to an emergency. My brother-in-law from Calgary graciously returned for the last few days of October and the first week of November. We were delighted to be able to spend Halloween with my son and his family. He and I were able to pick up my mom from the airport when she flew in from Edmonton for the second week of November, and we had a wonderful time enjoying each other's company. I was grateful for my family in Edmonton, who got my mom to and from the airport. My daughter left her 13-month-old son with his dad, so she could stay with me on Remembrance Day weekend. She took my mom back to the airport early Saturday morning. We went out for lunch with my mom's sister, her husband, and their daughter the day before. I have a fabulous picture of my mom, daughter, aunt, uncle, and cousin at the Cactus Club in Vancouver. My aunt and uncle from Abbotsford were very supportive financially and lent my brother-in-law their car. After my daughter left on

Chapter 9

Sunday, November 13, 2016, I was by myself for several days, and my son dropped in to visit a few times. I will never forget that part of my journey and thank all my family members and friends for playing an instrumental role in my recovery.

My husband arrived on Thursday evening November 17th and accompanied me to an appointment first thing Friday morning. We spent the weekend together, and I had an appointment with the transplant clinic on Monday, November 21st. We were ecstatic when the doctor on duty gave us the green light to go home. It was another bittersweet moment, packing up our belongings and leaving Stacey house, our family's home away from home for the previous two months.

The next phase began—healing at home. Once there, I realized I was still on the mend and physically very weak. I had no energy to do very much and took several naps a day. My husband cooked the Christmas dinner because I could not stand for very long. I went to the clinic to get my bandage changed on the drain every week until March 2017. It took many months to regain my strength, and I likely went too far the first time I went for a walk. Even though I moved at a snail's pace, I had to stop at a coffee shop to rest.

As I got stronger and stronger, I was able to meet friends for lunch, dinner, or coffee, and my husband continued to drive me because I didn't get the okay to drive until a visit to the transplant clinic on May 5, 2017. I was grateful my license was not suspended and that I only stopped driving under my doctor's advisement. I asked one of my friends, a driving instructor, to take me out on a road test. She assured me I had the confidence and skills to drive again.

A group of my work friends knew my husband had been living between Stacey House and our mobile home, and they wanted to give us the gift of a clean home for Christmas. When

I first received their email, I didn't want to have them in my mobile home because I compared their houses to ours. At the time, my definition was that we lived in a trailer on a gravel road on indigenous land. It was a lesson in humility because I later realized how blessed I was to have such wonderful friends who came over on a Sunday afternoon on the 18th of December to clean my house and set up my Christmas tree. They brought their own cleaning supplies, coffee, and love. I will be eternally grateful for the lesson, the help, and the opportunity to reframe my definition of my home to *I live in a mobile home in the country with a million-dollar view of the Saanich Inlet without the million-dollar price tag.*

My father-in-law was one of 13 children, and their family had incredible adventures with their siblings and families. There were many years when we lived in Alberta, and we attended a family camp-out in the summer, a Rachar women's retreat in the fall, and a Rachar Christmas celebration. The Christmas party always had a theme, skits, singing, Santa Claus, presents, and usually a turkey dinner with all the fixings. My father-in-law's nieces and nephews took turns putting on the Christmas event each year. While I was recovering at home in December 2016, my brother and sister-in-law from Edmonton oversaw the annual event. They chose to have a silent auction to allow aunts, uncles, and cousins the opportunity to support me through my recovery by raising money for me. My brother-in-law created an amazing sign detailing my journey each step of the way. He even drew a red liver with an arrow pointing to it with its new name, *Oliver*. We thanked everyone who contributed and my brother and sister-in-law for their thoughtfulness in creating the silent auction.

It took several years to recover from the second liver transplant, and I was scheduled for a follow-up appointment

Chapter 9

every six months. A friend told me about a refuge, Honour House, a home away from home for members of the Canadian Armed Forces, veterans, emergency services personal, and their families, where we could stay free of charge while receiving medical treatment in Vancouver. We were grateful we could stay at Honour House and visit our son, daughter-in-law, and grandchildren. In March 2017, I started to show signs of rejection. It was detected in my routine blood work, so I went back to Vancouver for a liver biopsy and then to the hospital in Victoria for high doses of prednisone, which were given intravenously over several days.

We didn't visit Alberta often, and when we did, it was like a speed-dating game or a bit like musical chairs. We did our best to divide our time between our family during a short two-to-three-day visit. One of my nieces had Crohn's disease and was diagnosed with cancer. She only had a few months to live, so we planned a trip to Alberta for Easter 2017 and intended to visit her and her family in Calgary for a few hours. I was super excited because I hadn't seen her for several years. Unfortunately, a few days before we started our trip, I discovered an itchy rash under my left breast. I made an appointment with my doctor, who diagnosed me with a milder case of shingles. As a result, I couldn't visit my niece and her family. I called her the day before and expressed how disappointed I was.

We learned she was in the palliative care unit at the Foothills Medical Center in Calgary a few months later. We knew she only had a short time on this Earth, and with every fibre of my being, I wanted to get on a plane and hold her in my arms to say goodbye. I couldn't do that for several reasons, so I asked myself what I could do. I decided to call her husband and ask him to hold the phone up to her ear so I could say, *I love you and will miss you terribly.* It was the first time I said goodbye to a loved one and the hardest words I ever spoke into a phone.

When I came home from the hospital in late November 2016, we had enormous credit card debt, a mortgage and car payment. It had nothing to do with the medical expenses associated with the transplants because we were blessed with all the financial support we received along the way. This mess was created before the transplants. Here I was, 60 years old, recovering from a second transplant, and I had to ask myself *When the fudge was I going to learn the lessons I needed about money.* I recognized I needed to voice my intentions and set some boundaries for eliminating our debt if I wanted to speak my truth and live life on my terms.

So, with my retirement looming, I booked an appointment with a counsellor and told her I was overwhelmed and stressed about our financial situation. She suggested that both my husband and I come in for an appointment. I left her office feeling nervous, not knowing what I might say to my husband. However, I also knew I had reached the end of my rope; my co-dependant days were over. If I was going to stay married, we needed to do something significantly different to change our financial situation.

I learned that when you know better, you do better, so I decided to tell my husband that if he wanted to continue this adventure with me, we needed to eliminate our debt before I turned 65. At this point, we were married over 45 years and had never gone to a counsellor together, so we didn't know what to expect. Fortunately, it was the best decision we made for both of us and our relationship. It wasn't a piece of cake, but it gave us a great foundation to talk about our situation and make plans to get out of debt. We created budgets, researched debt elimination strategies, created a plan, and just three months after I turned 65, we got rid of all our credit card debt, paid off our car, and for the first time in our marriage, we were able to save money every month.

We shifted our old patterns and ways of communicating around money and now have a much healthier relationship in our retirement years. We changed our habits and beliefs around nutrition and exercise. My husband released over one hundred pounds, and I learned to eat when and what was best for my body. I have eliminated sugar, dairy, beef, and pork from my diet. My husband follows a whole food plant-based diet, and we get plenty of fresh air and exercise. We are both living a healthier lifestyle post-transplant. Being married for many years gave me the opportunity to fall in love with my husband at least seven times. We are truly blessed that we found each other and have worked on our communication skills, grown personally together, and weathered our storms.

While working for the federal government, I noticed I put on a game face at work. A friend and I always had a meeting at the beginning of the year to set goals for the year and decide how we wanted to show up in every area of our life. I realized that no one at work really knew who I was, and I desired to be more authentic but didn't know how. I always loved quotes and found they could change my perspective as food for thought. Since I worked in a pod and had a whiteboard outside my wall, I got the idea to show up early every morning and write a quote on the board. It didn't take long before staff members walked by my desk and saw the quote of the day. I received emails from staff members thanking me for helping them change their perspective and inspiring them to think differently.

At some point during my years of service, I noticed a LOA—leave of absence—beside someone's name on a staff list. Several weeks or months later, I was curious if they had returned to work and noticed their name was no longer on the list. This left me wondering where they went, if they had passed away, decided to retire, or left the federal government altogether. I knew I did not want this to be me— someone, who faded away into the woodwork, with people asking where I was and what happened to me.

Due to some side effects from the anti-rejection medications, I began having trouble with concentration, memory, word mix-ups, and difficulty retaining information and making complex cognitive decisions. When I talked to my doctor in July 2017, she referred me to a neurologist, who I saw in January 2018. My test results gave him cause for alarm, and he diagnosed me with objective cognitive dysfunction. He suggested I have a full neuropsychological assessment and ordered one through the public healthcare system. He thought this could take 18 to 24 months. On top of this, due to pre and post-transplant symptoms, I had several hernias and was waiting for an operation. I was unable to bend or climb and was limited to walking or standing for no longer than 15 to 30 minutes.

I then received a letter from my employer indicating I had been off work since March 21, 2016, and I needed to decide by March 9, 2018, whether I could return to work. The company that administered the disability benefit with my employer had a policy requiring an employee to either return to work or retire at the two-year mark of a leave. Since my position had been challenging and I was experiencing cognitive dysfunction, I was deathly afraid of having to return to work. I booked an appointment with the same counsellor I saw previously, and she gave me the best advice I use to this day—I had to go through the process one step at a time. Basically, I needed to do what I could with what I had from where I was. I proceeded to

Chapter 9

make phone calls, set up appointments, and ask for help. One of my dear friends had gone through the process of leaving work due to a disability and she was a great resource. Due to the unsolved issues that could have taken another six months to a year to sort out, I chose to retire.

The day came when I needed to pick a retirement date and sign a letter. Since I knew I wanted closure as a public servant and with my career, I asked the manager if I could come back to work to say goodbye. I didn't think this had ever been done because most people pass away, move, or aren't well enough to return. I was courageous and asked because I knew that I wouldn't be able to look at myself in the mirror if I didn't. I let the manager know I didn't want a big party or send-off.

The date was set, and, of course, they surprised me with a gathering of most of the people I worked with over my fifteen-year career. I completely surprised myself by going around the room and hugging every single person. Thank goodness it was pre-COVID, otherwise it wouldn't have been possible to make this connection. I was able to speak directly from my heart and even added some unexpected humour. The manager gave a short speech indicating I had left a legacy and made a difference with my daily quotes. He shared that many staff members appreciated the daily quotes and asked if someone else could continue to post them in various places around the office.

I retired on medical leave on August 18, 2018, and I spent the first few years healing, writing, taking courses, volunteering, and creating more new habits. I also looked after my grandson on many occasions until March 2020. When I think back to those days in the ICU and all the health issues that needed sorting out, I didn't realize how sick I was before the operation, and I now realize *I've come a long way, baby.* I had lost my physical strength and confidence, but I didn't lose my vision to get well—my vision to watch my grandchildren grow up and see myself healthy and strong. I know there wasn't just one thing that made the difference in improving my health, my finances, or relationships but rather doing a few small things consistently over time. It is remembering and contemplating the Serenity prayer by Reinhold, *God grant me the serenity to accept the things I cannot change, the courage to change the things I can, and the wisdom to know the difference.*

Chapter 9

My Recipe for Recovery being a Team Effort

- *Karma—what goes around, comes around;*
- *Have a vision of recovery and return to health;*
- *Be present in the moment—***here** *is no better than* **there***;*
- *Be grateful every day for everything and everyone;*
- *Go through the process;*
- *Healing is an act of faith;*
- *Listen to my body's wisdom;*
- *Show up authentically at work.*

My Self-Reflection

While I was in the hospital, I believe my kindness, compassion, and caring were reflected in the kind of love, care, and support I received. I showed up authentically, remembered people's names, listened, and remembered everyone was doing their best. When I look back on my journey, I think having two liver transplants may have been the best thing that could have happened. I had the opportunity to deepen my relationship with my husband, family, and friends and change my relationship with money. I eliminated as much negativity as possible, remembered to listen to my body, had faith and visualized myself fully recovered. I continue to keep a gratitude journal and remind myself there is no better place than here. The grass is not greener on the other side of the fence. There is so much I do not understand about being human, and I realize it is impossible to understand everything. It is impossible to know why things happen the way they do; I believe they are part of life. Was needing to have two liver transplants a good thing? Maybe and maybe not. However, it happened, and I'm more humble, physically and mentally stronger, and more aware of who I am because I did.

Chapter 9

What is Your Recipe For Recovery being a Team Effort?

Evolving To Be Me

Given Your Recipe, Share Your Self-Reflection

X

Trusting Myself; The Final Chapter

The essence of trust is believing you will be held up if you let go.

~ Mark Nepo

Once I returned home, I realized I needed to create a new schedule and morning routine. Although it did take some time to recover, I wanted to reinvent myself, so to speak. What did I like to do? What brought me joy? What new habits did I want to commit to? What habits and tasks did I want to include in my daily schedule? I developed an excel spreadsheet with about ten items to track my progress. I read many books about time management and creating new habits. The two most impactful books were, *Make Time: How to Focus on What Matters Every Day* by Jake Knapp and John Zeratsky and *Atomic Habits* by James Clear. For the first year, recording my temperature, blood pressure, and weight every morning was part of my morning routine. I added simple things like brushing my teeth and getting dressed as if I was going to work—no sweats or t-shirts. I went for a walk, even if it was to the mailbox and back, wrote in a gratitude journal, and kept track of what I was eating. I also connected with someone every day and watched or listened to something inspiring. This helped me keep my spirits up and get the sense I had accomplished something.

On December 31, 2019, China alerted the World Health Organization to cases of an unusual pneumonia in Wuhan, now known as the coronavirus or COVID-19. On February 5, 2020, my husband and I flew to Edmonton for a sock-hop hosted by my brother and sister-in-law, and news of the coronavirus was on all the televisions in the airport. I noticed that my attitude at the time was that *it's over there and doesn't affect me*. How often do I have that thought? I have changed my perspective since then and believe everything affects everyone.

On March 10, 2020, the World Health Organization announced a COVID-19 global pandemic. The protocols put in place had a significant impact on how I lived from that day forward. Several years later, many restrictions have been lifted, and my perception is that people sense things are getting back to normal, and they can breathe a sigh of relief. More than ever, during times of uncertainty, I believe in showing love, being tolerant, and providing compassion to my fellow humans. I had some fear and frustration, and I noticed some uncertainty. However, I reminded myself that nothing is good or bad in life; my reaction makes the difference. The meaning I place on an event is what gives it power over me and makes it either good or bad. How I treat others and show up in the world is a choice. I can choose courage, bravery, and kindness and use the knowledge and information available at my fingertips more than ever before.

On March 26, 2020, I wrote a blog post about how I viewed the pandemic as an opportunity to recalibrate. Recalibrating means changing the way one thinks or does something. I am most familiar with this term from our car's old global positioning system when it said, *Recalibrating* when I drove in a different

Chapter 10

direction than instructed. This quote by Charles Darwin sums it up, *It is not the strongest of the species that survives but the most adaptable.*

I know what a difference a day makes...even a few minutes or hours. I was aware my emotions were heightened when I became uncertain about what changes to make to navigate the pandemic and how my life might look different. I reflected on my diagnosis, my transplant, and my recovery, and an old familiar feeling washed over me. *I've got this.* I have the skills and ability to recalibrate and make self-care a priority by focusing on two things. The first is determining what I can and cannot control. The second is to figure out what I have and what, if anything, is missing. I changed the way I thought and created new habits and behaviours. I adapted to my new environment and used technology and social media to connect with family and friends and meet new people. My husband and I developed a more meaningful connection because we needed to have new conversations about my health risk due to a compromised immune system.

I've learned that I could navigate my outer world by healing my inner world. In doing so, I can now observe my thoughts and what I create. I noticed my emotions and what I perceive on a daily basis. Healing myself is so much more than healing my body; it is also about healing my mind and spirit.

Several weeks after the announcement, my husband and I were out walking when I heard myself say, *When this is over...* It doesn't even matter what I said after that because my life is in the now—at this present moment. As often as I remember, I tell myself, *I am here now.* During the pandemic, I asked myself, *What will I do when self-isolating, social distancing, and staying at home are a thing of the past? What can I do now? What am I waiting for?* I wrote out a list of things I wanted to do when the pandemic was over. I asked myself, *What is on this list that I can do today or right now?*

I realized I was unconsciously waiting for the pandemic to be over, so I could see or communicate with my grandchildren. Because of this technological age, I discovered I could set up a schedule with my grown children to have a FaceTime chat with my grandchildren. It has been one of the most meaningful ways to spend my time. I am grateful I have the freedom and technology to continue having and developing meaningful relationships with my family and friends.

Having new habits, schedules, and morning and evening routines helped me navigate the last two years with optimism. I discovered what was most important, what brought me joy, and how I wanted to spend my time. I learned from my hospital journey to limit as much drama and negativity as possible. I didn't forget my early lesson that my life changes from the books I read, the people I spend time with, and the information I feed my mind.

There were times when I started to feel as restricted as I did in the hospital. Once again, I had to remind myself that I have the freedom to choose my thoughts and feelings and the kind of action I take on any given day. Changing my surroundings makes a difference, like being outside in nature, taking a drive, or connecting with others. Although I have a compromised immune system and seeing people face to face poses a health risk, I focus on what I can do. During the first year of the pandemic, a highlight was visiting my lab technician, who was very kind by coming to my car to draw blood to protect me. I was so excited to see her and have a few precious minutes sitting beside and chatting with a live person. This awareness taught me to focus on what I can do to enjoy every moment of the daily gifts I am given. There is always something to be

Chapter 10

grateful for and look forward to, even if it's getting a routine blood test.

I protect my mental health by connecting with others and engaging in activities like writing, meditating, listening to music, and spending time in nature. I also volunteer, eat, and hydrate well, and get plenty of exercise. I have a joy list and make sure to do several things on it every day. I am a lifelong learner, and I want to challenge myself by trying new things, joining different groups, and meeting new people.

About a year after my recovery, I started sharing quotes with people via Facebook messenger, email, and phone messages. Similar to when I was working and posted quotes on my white board. My intention is to brighten someone's day and give them food for thought. When I returned home, I started writing a memoir about my liver transplant journey and didn't seem to have the confidence to finish it. I let my inner critic, fears, and insecurities prevent me from completing it. Then I came across this quote by Cyril Connolly, *Better to write for yourself and have no public, than to write for the public and have no self.* I believed this quote was speaking directly to me, *I MUST write this book for myself, for having No Self is not an option!* Speaking from my heart is what matters most and makes me human. It matters not that anyone hears me, for when I speak from my heart, I notice my spirit soar.

While isolating over the first eleven months of the pandemic without interacting with others in person, I developed a comfort zone but feared my world was shrinking. There is a saying, *When the student is ready, the teacher appears* by Buddha Siddhartha Guatama Shakyamuni. I am so grateful a friend introduced me to one of the coaches and authors of a wonderful workbook and process, *Daring to Share Your Story, An Authentic Writing Guide* by Diana Reyers and Tana

Heminsley because I was a student who was ready to be taught. I purchased this step-by-step workbook in February 2021 and followed the process to write this memoir. As I went through each step, I recognized I hadn't always trusted myself, and by following this guide, I uncovered old patterns and began to understand how my childhood shaped my beliefs, thoughts, and stories. Writing my memoir in this way helped me trust myself, believe I am worthy, and validate that I am enough.

Learning the effects of growing up around an alcoholic helped me understand why I haven't trusted myself, especially when taking on new projects. It is normal for adult children of alcoholics to develop serious trust issues. I've discovered that women who grow up as an adult child of an alcoholic often become fixers, and it was especially true for me because I was the eldest daughter. My need to fix things became so strong that I had difficulty having fun. I didn't know how to play, relax, or choose *being* versus *doing*. Being aware of that truth about myself helped me lighten up, not take life so seriously, laugh at myself, and occasionally shake my sillies out! I now truly love and accept myself, and the bonus is that I am having more fun.

I have been practising meditation, and although I am not a master at it, it helps me to gain clarity and tap into inner peace. Several months ago, I completed a new moon meditation and got in touch with my inner child. I asked her what she wanted more of, and she whispered, *Play, fun, dance, exploration, and rest*. My mind flashed back to an incident many years ago in Alsask, Saskatchewan, where I saw my inner child in her bliss, laughing, playing, and exploring life until my dad released all his anger on her. I realized she was still with me at that moment, and I needed to remember who she was and still is. When I was that version of myself with my friend, we explored, ran, jumped, and loved the sun on our faces and the connection we had. I realized it was one of the happiest days of my life, but I had blocked it out due to an old perception. It wasn't wrong to be experiencing bliss without a care in the world while having fun. My feelings were real, they were mine, and they were not gone; I could allow them to resurface any time.

When I started the Daring to Share process, it was a new exercise for me. I found myself wanting to read someone else's story to see if I was doing it right before I started. I realized this was an old pattern of thinking and something I defaulted to when learning something new. So, I asked myself some questions: *Why do I need to see someone else's work? Is it because I can then do it like them and get a decent mark or grade? Where does this feeling come from, and why don't I trust myself?*

I knew being vulnerable was the best next step, so I posted a question in the Facebook Group which was created by one of the book's co-authors, Diana Reyers, asking for clarification. I recognized that there were times in the past when I had soldiered on and kept working because I was afraid of embarrassing myself. I often compared myself to someone else and didn't give myself a chance. I got clarification, guidance, and excellent support and realized part of the process was to trust my intuition, heart, and soul to write honestly about my perceptions, thoughts, and emotions.

As I continued to work through the writing process, I recognized my old thought patterns and the feeling of being overwhelmed. Once I was aware of this, I was able to ask myself what my soul was saying to me, *Trust yourself, Debra—your body, mind, and spirit. This is your life. Be curious, speak your truth, find your voice, and share who you are with the world. Spread your wings and fly.* Then, the thought came up, *Who would I be without my story?* This is a modification of the title of a Byron Katie book, *Who would you be without your story?* So, I delved deeper and asked, *What am I continuing to tell myself that isn't true? What am I telling myself that keeps me from living my authentic life?*

Once I recognized that I haven't always trusted myself, I wanted to clarify how I knew when to trust myself as well as recognize when I don't trust myself. In addition to growing up in a dysfunctional environment, I also noticed that several people, exposures, and events could have prevented me from trusting myself. I relied heavily on others, educational institutions, my boss, and my working environment. My career mainly consisted of administrative support roles, and I was given training and a job description that didn't require trusting my intuition. This career also seemed to fit my recipe mentality.

Being co-dependent for many years meant relying on a pattern of allowing my husband to make many decisions. Once I unravelled these behaviour patterns, thoughts, and feelings, I realized my most important lesson from this process was to trust myself and my intuition. I also needed to complete my memoir; after all, it's my story so, how could it be wrong?

I became aware that I gain a sense of pride when I trust my intuition and follow through. Anything I have chosen to do has been fueled with the idea of personal growth, expansion, and becoming a better person. My underlying intention is and has been personal growth when I create relationships, volunteer, take courses, or join network marketing companies. I always asked, *How can I become a better human being, and what action can I take to be proud of myself?*

I now know my inner voice is my intuition, and it is a guidepost or compass for how I want to show up in the world. I watched a YouTube interview with Tom Bilyeu and Susan David and reflected on Tom Bilyeu's punch line that *Life is how you feel about yourself when you are by yourself.* My soul whispered the word, *proud.*

Chapter 10

What is my soul trying to tell me? I'm here, listening. *Stop, just stop trying so hard. You are perfect the way you are—making any kind of a mistake does not mean you are not good enough. It's an old thought pattern.* By participating in the Daring to Share My Story process, I learned to trust myself, listen to my intuition—my soul—and speak my truth. What I've learned is that: *For pride to work, it must be paired with humility — a humility to know that no matter our skill set, each of us depends on what others have to offer. Since none of us can be an expert in all areas, we must be humble enough to recognize that we cannot be great at everything; there will be times when we need to rely on others. People who follow this advice are the ones for whom pride, like gratitude and compassion, becomes a virtue, not a vice.*[21]

My niece, Rena Rachar,[22] who is a life coach, gave me an invaluable tool entitled, *What Am I Feeling?* I label my deepest feelings on a wheel and then get in touch with them. I was programmed to shove mine down and block them out. Several months ago, I labelled a feeling as abandonment, and I immediately wanted to distract myself by reaching out to someone. That way, I wouldn't have to acknowledge that emotion. If I continued this behaviour, I could be running away from looking inward to determine what is really going on. Through the Daring to Share process, I learned to focus on taking care of myself emotionally, spiritually, and physically, trust myself, label my emotions, and show up as my authentic self.

I asked myself, *How do I build trust with others?* And answered, *When they do what they say they will do and when they clearly communicate their thoughts and feelings to me. What*

---

[21] https://ideas.ted.com/pride-can-be-a-virtue-but-it-needs-to-be-the-right-kind-of-pride/
[22] renarachar.com

motivates me to trust my husband? I answered, *His behaviour towards me, his actions, and our deep connection and commitment to our marriage.* I trust him with my life! *What is different with my relationship with myself? Do I keep commitments to myself?*

I was honest when I answered, *Not always*. However, I am becoming more focused, less distracted, and more committed to myself. *Do I communicate my thoughts and feelings to myself? Do I listen, or do I dismiss my emotions to get something done? Am I a human who is doing?* I love this quote by Stephen R. Covey, *Making and keeping promises to ourselves precedes making and keeping promises to others.* I've learned to trust the people around me, trust the flow of life, and trust myself. I always ask myself, *What role did I play in this situation? And did I take responsibility for the options and choices I have or had?*

A habit I am overcoming is resistance. I had some resistance in leaving my job, retiring from my career, writing my memoir, and believing there was a pandemic at the beginning of COVID-19. I didn't realize I carried a belief that if I couldn't see it with my eyes, it didn't exist. I started to wonder what was happening around me or internally that I was resisting. Resistance in always present and showed up in many ways. When I was sick in the hospital and recovering from surgery, sometimes I resisted eating and exercising. It was and is my choice to overcome resistance to ensure I look after my body, mind, and spirit. Resistance continues to show up each day, and I have the option to either give in to it or overcome it. I choose to overcome it every day. As a writer, I know I must write every day. I learned the purpose of writing is to express myself and allow my inner voice to be released on paper; to sing my song through my written words, be creative, express my soul, and allow my spirit to flow. I love this quote by Steven Pressfield, *All that matters is I've put in my time and hit it with all I've got.*

Chapter 10

All that counts is that, for this day, for this session, I have overcome Resistance.

As I continue to detect and label my feelings, get in touch with who I am, keep commitments to myself, and know I am enough I reflect on this quote by Pema Chödrön, *What you do for yourself, any gesture of kindness, any gesture of gentleness, any gesture of honesty and clear seeing toward yourself, will affect how you experience your world. In fact, it will transform how you experience the world. What you do for yourself, you're doing for others, and what you do for others, you're doing for yourself.*

I have had many wonderful encounters and received new lessons since the pandemic. I had the opportunity to attend weekly Zoom calls with Jon Kabat-Zinn to listen to his wisdom and heal. It was life-altering and supported me to see the world in many different ways. I learned to choose to be grateful for everything I have, for all I have earned and worked for. I now fill my mind with gratitude for all beings and all things. He also talked about viewing any life event as part of the curriculum. I understood what he meant firsthand and knew it had become part of my deliberate thought pattern in November of 2020. It was an ordinary day, and I was driving to one of my favorite places to pick up some buns when, *Bam,* someone ran into the back of my SUV. I didn't realize I had been hit until the person at On-Star asked if I had been in an accident. It was then that I realized a Red Dodge Ram truck had hit me from behind at 30 kilometres an hour while I was stopped for pedestrians crossing the street. The thought that ran through my mind was, *I guess this is my curriculum.* Attending those Zoom calls gave me the tools to be calm, emotionally intelligent, and authentic in all situations, even in a car accident.

Fortunately, I was not injured badly because the seat belt deployed and held me in the seat. However, I chose to go to the hospital by ambulance to get checked out, and on the way to the hospital, the paramedic asked me how I could stay so calm, and I said, *I practice mindfulness and meditation.* He may have thought I was looney if I had said, *The car accident was my curriculum.* I handled the process one step at a time. Our vehicle was written off, and I believe by being calm, acting in the areas I could, and believing in a positive outcome, I ended up getting the proper medical attention and eventually finding the right replacement vehicle.

It was an afternoon in late December, after Christmas but before New Year's, and my husband and I were purchasing a vehicle through a private sale, something we begrudged doing in the middle of a pandemic. We sent a text to the seller when we arrived and proceeded to wait in the backyard for her to appear. We knew that she was selling her father's vehicle because he was very ill and didn't have long to live. The vehicle was parked right outside the door of her father's suite. Was I anxious and wondering where she was? Was I impatient or judgemental? No, I decided to be present at the moment and look for the magic in her backyard. I wondered what I might hear, sense, see, or smell while waiting for the seller? I reminded myself that I have lots of time, unlike the seller, who has a limited number of precious moments left with her dad. I opened my eyes in wonder when I saw a pair of squirrels running across the yard and then scampering up a tree. I heard children laughing in the near distance as they played in a playground close by. I smelled the dirt in the flowerpots as it soaked up the rainwater that had fallen the night before. I touched the soft fur of the big orange cat that sauntered over to get some love. I was swept away by the wonder that surrounds me every day when I take the time to stop, look, and listen for it.

The time flew by, and I can't say how many minutes passed

before the seller came out of her home with the necessary paperwork for us to sign. I was in a place of gratitude and compassion and asked her to let her father know how grateful we were to have his vehicle. In that precious moment, we both knew we were doing something we begrudged. This inspired me to continue asking myself, *Where is the magic in this moment?*

During this last year I learned I had a fear of missing out. In the past, I have purchased a plethora of online courses and books and attended thousands of Zoom calls and webinars. Prior to my transplant, I was completing morning pages which is a practice shared by Julia Cameron in her book *The Artist's Way*. I returned to this practice once I was well enough, and it is part of my morning routine. I chose to gain clarity by writing about my fear of missing out. Once I recognized the fear and could label it, I could identify the teachings I resonated with and wanted to listen to. Several months later, a friend approached me about taking another online course. I confidently declined because it didn't resonate with me, and I no longer have the fear of missing out.

My hunger for adventure, variety, and excitement has gotten me in over my head many times. I now slow down, gracefully say no, and take the time to gain clarity. Most important to me is having a good relationship with my husband, children and grandchildren and spending time with my friends and family. For me, happiness is a matter of attitude, attention, and intention. I take the time to thank the sun for shining, and I buy myself flowers and appreciate the joy of being a spiritual being having a human experience.

I have discovered that I possess the positive characteristics of an adult child of an alcoholic, which include resilience, empathy, maturity, responsibility, sensitivity, and drive. There

Evolving To Be Me

is a flip side to the laundry list,[23] and I believe I have worked through the characteristics I learned as a child and let them go. Now I know that:

- I no longer fear others, including authority figures and have moved away from feeling isolated;
- I no longer depend on others to tell me who I am;
- Angry people do not frighten me, and I am not threatened by personal criticism;
- I live my life from the standpoint of authenticity rather than victimhood;
- Having enabling behaviours no longer prevents me from looking at my shortcomings;
- Setting boundaries has become easier, and I no longer detect guilt for voicing my truth;
- I choose relationships that inspire me, and I intend to inspire others. No Drama!
- I am starting to come out of denial to regain the ability to label and express my emotions;
- I judge myself a lot less and have discovered a sense of self-worth;
- I have interdependent relationships with healthy people and those who are emotionally available;
- The characteristics of alcoholism and para-alcoholism that have been internalized are identified, acknowledged, and removed;
- I can act maturely in all situations and no longer react negatively.

---

[23] https://adultchildren.org/literature/laundry-list/

Chapter 10

Until now, I have not completely understood why I developed the characteristics I unknowingly did as a child. Yet, I'm grateful I have had the patience and persistence to heal from those characteristics to survive. Perhaps my purpose was to learn how to overcome the traits of conflict avoidance, codependency, fear of unworthiness, and the belief that whatever happened was my fault, and I needed to fix it.

I'm learning to be more grateful, develop a positive attitude, and really appreciate all the beauty around me every day. It's about how I show up in the world and how well I take care of my mind, body, and spirit. There is an abundance of love, joy, and laughter all around. I can create abundance, and there are opportunities to be of service and to share my gifts everywhere. For me, abundance doesn't only encompass money and possessions but rather having faith and trust in a higher power that there is enough, I am enough, and whatever I want is available to me. As a child, whatever I was taught became my reality until I decided to change it. These days, my dominant perspective in life is abundance. I have learned to trust in the world around me, and, although it has taken me some time to get here, I know I can trust that all things are working out for me in every way every day. Therefore, I choose to continue to grow and change and look deeper when things don't turn out as I expected; I ask myself, *What am I here to learn?*

I have new coping skills to cultivate healthier relationships and have developed an improved sense of self-worth and self-esteem. I have taken off my game face to show up authentically in all areas of my life. Two final quotes by Susan David, *Discomfort is the price of admission for a meaningful life.* And *Courage is fear walking.*

My Recipe For Trusting Myself

- *Keeping commitments to myself builds trust and raises my self-esteem;*
- *Recalibrate—change how I think and do things;*
- *My life is now—what am I waiting for?*
- *Change my definition of freedom;*
- *When the student is ready, the teacher appears;*
- *Whatever I am faced with is my curriculum;*
- *Learn to trust myself and let go of resistance;*
- *Learn to recognize my childhood traits and flip them around.*

My Self-Reflection

My encounters have taught me that life is a journey, not a destination. The past does not equal the future, and life happens for me, not to me. How I respond or react to life's challenges determines if I learn from them. I'm proud of myself for detecting the childhood behaviours I carried into adulthood and changing old beliefs, stories, and patterns of thinking. What helped me is knowing I have been resilient and continued to find renewed energy to pick myself up, dust myself off, and get on with the next adventure. I can now view life as an adventure, and I can look at setbacks as an opportunity to create new plans, look at new possibilities, and ways to help others. My two most important commodities are my mind and energy. I choose what I put into my mind and learn new ways to create more energy. I can only connect the dots looking backwards and have noticed that they indeed connect. I have

Chapter 10

learned valuable lessons along the way, including that life is a practice. I practice creating good habits while becoming more authentic and courageous. I communicate from love, not fear, and continue to label my feelings and be aware of my thoughts and how my energy affects others. I speak my truth, prioritize self-care, and spend more time *being* versus *doing*. I was given this one precious life, and what I do with it is up to me. I will continue to learn and grow until I say my final farewell to Mother Earth. I do not know how that will happen, but I'm going to live each day like it is an adventure.

What is Your Recipe For Trusting Yourself?

Chapter 10

Given Your Recipe, Share Your Self-Reflection

About the Author

Since her early twenties, Debra Rachar has been on a quest to learn how to be the best possible version of herself. She shares how she overcame the characteristics she learned from growing up with an alcoholic parent. Once she discovered her co-dependant behaviour patterns, she could become interdependent. Debra knew she had to change her thought patterns, beliefs, and stories and that she possessed positive traits carried inside her. She believes she survived two liver transplants within 25 days by changing her behaviour and recognizing her positive attributes.

When Debra isn't spending time with her husband, family, or friends, she can be found writing blog posts for her newsletter, *Food for Thought*, journaling, or volunteering by checking in on seniors. She has been sharing quotes for several years to inspire others to see things differently and lift their spirits.

Debra shares her struggles, lessons, emotions, and recipes to encourage others to believe the past does not equal the future. She hopes you find yourself somewhere in her story and become inspired to find your voice, accept that you are enough, you are worthy, and you can evolve to become your authentic self.